'If your aliveness is missing or defunct, Eloise Skinner's book will help you reclaim it. A practical yet deeply rich guide that facilitates your creation of a fulfilling work-life portfolio through the examination of mind, body, work, and self.'

Dan Pontefract, award-winning author of *Work-Life Bloom*, *Lead. Care. Win.*, and others

'Life is not so much about having the right answers as it is about asking the right questions. And a great one to begin with is: "But are you alive?" Eloise Skinner eloquently and beautifully explores this theme, pulling from her own deep exploration of spirituality, psychology, and the actual act of living. It is a brave, bold book you will want to read more than once. Don't let this book, and more importantly this question, go by without attempting to answer it.'

Jeff Goins, bestselling author of *The Art of Work*

'A rich, interesting book, especially important for those who feel they have lost their way. A valuable, modern book for a new generation.'

Dr Alfried Längle, M.D., Ph.D., founder of Existential Analysis, www.gle-uk.com

But Are You Alive?

How to Design a Life Worth Living

Eloise Skinner

JOHN MURRAY

First published by John Murray One in 2023
An imprint of John Murray Press
A division of Hodder & Stoughton Ltd,
An Hachette UK company

1

A CIP catalogue record for this title is available from the British Library

Trade Paperback ISBN 978 1 529 39 888 5
eBook ISBN 978 1 529 39 890 8

Typeset by KnowledgeWorks Global Ltd.

Printed and bound in Great Britain by Clays Ltd, Elcograf S.p.A.

John Murray Press policy is to use papers that are natural, renewable and recyclable products
and made from wood grown in sustainable forests. The logging and manufacturing processes
are expected to conform to the environmental regulations of the country of origin.

John Murray Press
Carmelite House
50 Victoria Embankment
London EC4Y 0DZ

www.johnmurraypress.co.uk

This book is dedicated to you, the reader – what a privilege to be part of your journey.

Contents

Aliveness

● ● ●

Life, these days, can be a little like walking into a huge supermarket.

You know the kind – the retail park supermarkets that stock *everything*, on multiple floors. At first, it's exciting: so many options! Stuff in all variations and colours! But, after a while, it can be exhausting. You get distracted. You forget what it was you were looking for. In amongst all the choice and the variety on offer, you can end up unfocused. And – at the risk of overextending the metaphor – sometimes the stuff you wanted was actually out of reach all along, even if it looked close enough to touch.

This feeling – of *existential overwhelm*, to give it a somewhat more dramatic title – isn't unique to shopping trips in huge supermarkets. Our modern lives contain a lot, both professionally and personally. At present, the median job tenure has fallen to 4.1 years,[1] and it's estimated that workers will have around 10–15 jobs in their lifetime.[2] And our personal lives are more diverse, too. For many of us, we've been encouraged to explore our passions and our purpose. We've been told – often through social media and online advertising – that we can define the life we want to live; we can choose our personal brand and 'side-hustles'; that we're creators and innovators and disruptors. (Whether this is true in a practical sense, of course, isn't always directly relevant: we can still get caught up in the overwhelm of choice and variety, even if we don't necessarily have the practical means to explore every option fully.) In some respects, we seem to be more free than ever to become the authors of our own existence.

But the endless choice on display can leave us unsettled. With so many things to do and tasks to achieve and options to pick, we can end up feeling like we don't know which way to turn. (This general kind of 'unanchored' feeling, in the psychological literature, is sometimes referred to as the 'existential vacuum',[3] a beautifully poetic way to describe a feeling of meaninglessness.) What are we *supposed* to do with our lives? Is there a right or wrong way of doing it? What happens if we move too slow, or too fast? Do we know what we want? Have we ever really thought about it?

All of this is, of course, exacerbated by social media: the push to present a perfect life on Instagram, a sparkling personal brand on LinkedIn, a consistent viewpoint on Twitter, and so on. And we do this to relax, in our 'free' time? No wonder we're all exhausted.

As for a solution, I'm not sure there is a single answer: in the end, I think we have to navigate our own paths. But I believe there's an alternative to the way we're often encouraged to live and work. I think it's possible for each of us to explore all the scattered elements of our existence, each so crucial for our sense of who we are, and bring them together to create a life that's fully integrated, fully unique and filled with meaning. In short, a life that's lived with full *aliveness*.

'Aliveness' isn't a word that lends itself to an easy or universal definition. Maybe the word makes you remember a particular time in your life when you really experienced a feeling of being fully alive, or perhaps it makes you think of a particular person who moves through the world with lightness, inspiration and joy. Either way, I'm sure you have your own assumptions about the term. Dictionary definitions of 'alive' often mention energy and vivacity, qualities that imply presence, fulfilment and drive. But as much as we can capture it with language and labels, the experience of being fully 'alive' is a personal one. Your sense of what it feels like to wake up each day with full *aliveness* will be different from mine. It's the kind of quality that doesn't allow itself to be ranked, rated, compared or measured: this is an individual journey, based on personal experience, heading towards a destination that only you can determine. We can simply say, to begin the work of this book, that 'aliveness' is an expansive, meaningful experience of life, one in which you feel present, driven and full of energy. The way this journey (towards greater 'aliveness') manifests on a practical level, or the way it feels on a personal level, or the methods you choose to utilize along the way – these are all elements for you to decide.

As I started studying the field of 'existential therapy',[4] I came across the term 'phenomenology' (from the Greek, generally translated as the study of 'that which appears'). Other than being a great word to use to impress your friends during casual conversation (*'Did I mention I've been reading about phenomenology?'*), the word captures an interesting approach, and one that we'll explore in our work together.[5] Phenomenology could be expressed as the attempt or effort to understand a thing as it is *in itself*, rather than trying to understand it through the framework of ideas or other ideologies. This approach takes a position of openness and non-judgement: it doesn't necessarily seek an answer, but instead looks for an *experience*. We could, perhaps, adopt this approach as a methodology: moving from the surface of things to a deeper pursuit of the 'essence' of the things we encounter. This attitude, as vague as it might sound, can come in helpful when we start to explore a sense of personal aliveness. As we work through each chapter, we'll be using questions like: *How* does it feel to experience this practice? *What* can this tell me? *What* did I like or dislike? We'll be looking at ourselves and our lives, trying to get beneath the surface, moving away from concrete answers and towards a lived experience of life. This approach can be challenging, at times, but you may also (as I have!) find it deeply rewarding.

For myself, this work – of becoming more 'alive' – has been my project over the last decade. And it's made my life challenging in a lot of ways. For one thing, it's taken me in and out of a range of careers: lawyer, author, teacher, dancer, existential therapist and even – briefly – a student in a monastic community (more on that later). In the pursuit of full 'aliveness', I've found it difficult to settle on one path. And, on a personal level, it can be exhausting. Phenomenology, existentialism, the meaning of life, trying to find your purpose – these topics are confronting, frustrating, and often yield no immediate results. The deeper you go, the more difficult it gets.

And then there's the question of whether we're entitled to be asking these types of questions at all (especially if, like me, you come at these topics without a financially-secure net to fall back on). It can feel risky to do this work, to move away from comfort and towards the unknown. And it often feels self-indulgent to be pondering our own existence. But, at the heart of it, these are questions that humans have been asking themselves, and each other, for millennia. How can we truly experience our fleeting moments on this planet? How can we live in such a way that the depth of our life becomes more meaningful than the length of it? How can we get to a position where we can look back at our journey and think: *yes*, that was my life, a life *I* created and designed, and a life I lived *fully*? In the end, this work is an enduring human tradition, an instinct and an impulse towards deeper 'aliveness'.

Joining that tradition, this book focuses on the idea of intentionally selecting, exploring and diving deeper into the central elements of your life. Throughout the chapters, you'll find a collection of teachings, traditions and actionable exercises, all designed to bring you closer to a full, meaningful experience of life. The practical approach is one of artistic experimentation: try things out, see how they land in your life, and feel free to change your mind or your routines at any point. This is your path, and it's up to you which direction you head in.

Together, we'll begin with an overview of our current landscape, and the circumstances we find ourselves in. We'll cover achievement culture, the burnout epidemic, and the wisdom of existential psychotherapy. And we'll touch on the unique time period we're currently moving through: the opportunities we have, in the coming years, to redefine our own lives, and the chances we have for new beginnings, approaches and perspectives. Next, we'll take a practical approach to the topic, exploring a toolkit for you to begin designing your own life. Moving through four major categories – Mind, Body, Work and Self – we'll travel through teachings, practices and exercises from a variety of traditions and backgrounds. And then, in the final section, I'll be handing over the pen, providing you with the steps you need to begin designing for yourself.

Later on in the book, we'll work with the concept of a 'portfolio', something that often arises in the context of creating a fulfilling *work* life. The work-related context is important – most people spend around a third of their lives working, after all. But this book takes the portfolio concept and extends it – to cover passion projects, identity, meaning, embodiment, relationships, connection, authenticity ... and much more. The fundamental idea, here, is the possibility of living at a deeper, more integrated level – going beneath the surface, figuring out how you really want to spend your time in the world, and then finding ways to shape and form your life accordingly. So, yes, this book is for anyone who feels lost, for anyone who feels like they're moving through life without purpose or direction or intention. But it's *also* for those who already know which way they're heading and just want to look for a little more depth along the way. It's a book that empowers you, the reader, to step into the role of creator – to form and shape your life according to your own unique design.

There's another aspect to this work, as well – an aspect closely connected to my own experience of success and achievement. It's been the case, on many occasions, that I've worked to achieve something, and when I finally reached it, I felt like it didn't live up to expectations. For many of us, this can be a central feature of our experience of life – working to get somewhere, or achieve something, only to find that it wasn't what we wanted, or it didn't fill the gap we were promised it would. And then, inevitably, there's a new goal or ambition, and the pursuit begins again.

I think an alternative path is possible. But it requires us, firstly, to re-evaluate our current lifestyles and assumptions, and then to begin the process of reorientating ourselves towards a more fulfilled, 'alive' experience, whatever that looks like in practice.

Over the last decade, I've been asked the same two questions hundreds of times. The first question, more straightforwardly, is: 'How do you do so many different things at once?' This is a question about time management, productivity, wellbeing and balance – topics I'll touch on in the course of this book. But a more interesting question is: '*Why* do you do so many different things at once?' This is a question about becoming more alive, about pursuing a life full of depth and meaning and purpose. Drawing on my experience across existentialism, spirituality, wellbeing, career development and psychotherapy, this book is my answer to that question.

PART I

The Landscape

CHAPTER 1

A Quick Look at Where We're At

• • •

If your life sometimes feels overwhelming or exhausting, you're not alone. In this chapter, we'll take a look at the social/cultural pressures for today's young adults, including changes in working patterns, social media, social expectations and much more. And, of course, we'll touch on the circumstances of the present moment, and the long-term shifts that might be heading our way in the years to come.

The pace of change

My first phone came with a daily allowance of ten text messages. Ten individual texts to send each day, to whoever I wanted. The allowance refreshed at midnight, so I'd have to predict the need for communication during the day, trying to make sure no message went to waste. Some days, around 11.30pm, there was an opportunity to get a little reckless with the remaining texts – send an emoticon,[1] perhaps. (Believe it or not, this was the world in 2005.)

We often think that change – in society, technology or culture – is achingly slow. We think things should be more advanced, or faster, or more efficient, or just *better* than the way they are today. Even a couple of hours without a good WiFi connection can leave us feeling disconnected and restless. On a day-to-day level, we tend not to reflect on the way things *used to be, back then*. But the acceleration of technology over the last decade has had a huge impact on the way we live. There are good things, of course – the deeper connections we can create; the globalization of our lives and work; the diversity of perspectives to learn from – but there are less good things, too. Some of these 'less good things' form central themes for the work of this book, and we'll touch on a few of them here.

1. BURNOUT (THE CURRENT EDITION)

These days, most of us are familiar with the concept of burnout. Perhaps you've even encountered it first-hand: the steady, enduring feeling of exhaustion that can seep into every aspect of your life. Burnout creeps up on you – one moment you're racing ahead, achieving goals, moving forwards; the next moment you're just moving through the motions, ticking off the exhausting elements of an endless to-do list. One of the most dangerous features of burnout is its subtlety – we can easily pass off a developing sense of burnout as tiredness or stress. We tell ourselves that we need a break, that things will be better when we reach the next hurdle. We promise ourselves a vacation once our next work project is completed. We wonder why we can't just 'pull it together' and gather the energy to do the things we once loved to do. The failure of these efforts, of course, can leave us even more demoralized than we were before.

Burnout is reported to be on the rise, too. Studies from 2021 show that, as we move into a post-pandemic world, a growing number of us are disillusioned and depleted.[2] But even as this reality becomes more visible, none of it is new. The term 'burnout' arrived into public discourse in the 1970s, developed by a German-born American psychologist and psychotherapist named Herbert Freudenberger. At this time, Freudenberger used the term to describe the consequences that resulted from his own high-pressured working environment, working in the fields of healthcare and addiction. Burnout, in this context, was characterized by a range of symptoms, including headaches, sleeplessness and 'quickness to anger'. Freudenberger noted the similarities to depression, too, writing that a worker encountering burnout 'looks, acts and seems depressed'. The difference between burnout and exhaustion, in many cases, is that exhaustion belongs to the present moment. We're exhausted *now*. But burnout reaches into the future and becomes a feature of our ongoing experience. We're 'burned out' for the long term.

Although we often associate burnout with the pressures of a working environment, the term today isn't limited to the consequences of a demanding job. Burnout can result from broader social pressures – expectations of others, comparisons to peer groups, the relentless demands of social media. And, importantly, burnout doesn't have to result from an exclusively negative set of circumstances. Burnout can happen when you're chasing your dreams, too. An inability to take breaks from your work; a feeling of never being able to 'get on top of things'; a sense that you'll never get a real rest – these are all features of burnout – and yet, they can happen in an environment that you've intentionally chosen for yourself, even one that you've dreamed of or passionately worked towards. Burnout doesn't make exceptions for situations in which you *feel as though* you should be thriving.

One central feature of the work we'll do in this book is a sense of 'disconnection' from the world. This is the feeling of standing outside of your own life, looking in on it, but somehow unable to participate fully. This feeling can manifest in a variety of ways, from a variety of sources, but burnout is a central example. Burnout keeps us at a distance from the richness of our own experience, preventing us from fully being able to be present. We end up too depleted to do the things we love, and we lose our sense of connection even to the things we are still able to do. Life, in a burned-out world, can seem clouded – a colourless experience, where everyday tasks begin to feel heavy. Burnout removes the shape and texture of our lives. The ups and downs of our emotions are dulled. Our experience of life becomes flat.

Clinical burnout is often best dealt with by quick intervention – making immediate changes in daily life, moving away from the direct cause of the burnout (if it can be identified), or starting a process of therapy or other supportive practice. This book is not a strategy for negotiating burnout, although it could be supportive within a long-term plan for burnout recovery. Instead of dealing with burnout's consequences, we're going to work on a set of tools, skills and abilities that might just steer us away from burnout before it begins. And, if burnout is something that comes our way, my hope is that this book provides you with the ability to observe your life as it shifts and changes, and gives you the creative authority to make meaningful changes where you can.

2. WELCOME TO THE INTERNET

Imagine a world with no global source of information at your fingertips. Imagine no notifications, no online ads, no scrolling, no swiping, no double tapping. This world used to exist, in the not-too-distant past. Back then, there were no constant news updates, unless you sought them out or happened to hear about them in person. No exposure to endless opinions of others, unless you looked for them, or read about them in print, or voluntarily chose to listen to someone expressing them. Maybe our lives were a little quieter (and harder in many different ways, of course, but a little less frantic).

For those of us who spend a good proportion of time on social media – for work or play or anything else – we know, intimately, that feeling of overwhelm. This societal leap, from in-person community interactions to exposure to an international scope of thought and opinion, is something we're not equipped to handle well. Even as mere observers, it can be draining to be in the midst of it all – debates and discussions and viral trends, all moving so fast that we can barely catch our breath. There are the undeniably negative elements: misinformation, hate, trolling, aggression, online bullying (none of this new to the human species, of course, but exacerbated by the accessibility and speed of our online environments). But even when we're talking about *good* things – online attention, growing audiences, going viral, visibility and appreciation – these things can be equally overwhelming. You can still be left exhausted and worn down by the pace of your online life, even if you have millions of adoring followers. Too much of a good thing can easily work against us.

When it comes to our lived experience, then, we end up in a similar position to the burnout example. From an existential perspective, we could say that both situations – burnout and overwhelm – separate us from the felt, lived experience of being human. But where burnout might lower our energy levels, forcing us away from participation in our lives, our online world can have the opposite effect. Instead of too little energy, we're constantly hyped, receiving more – information, opinions, perspectives – than we know what to do with. Our adrenaline is high before we've even unlocked our phones. It's difficult to know when (or how) to stop. And so, we skim over the depths of our daily lives in favour of something lighter; something clickable; something transient. Maybe we even lose sight of the possibility of depth altogether.

3. THE EMPTINESS OF SUCCESS

Many of us spent our early years with a predetermined sense of what it means to be successful. Whether we were listening to our parents, our teachers or any type of media, we usually figured out that money and power and beauty are some of the classic indicators of success. As we moved into adulthood, perhaps we added some more specific metrics. A job title. A mortgage. A long-term relationship. For many of us, this checklist may have actually formed a helpful template for figuring out what to do with our time. It becomes easier to pick out the perfect career path or lifestyle when there are some specific requirements to reach success. And then, somewhere along the way, many of us replaced the difficult, meandering path of getting to know our selves and our values with a more socially-acceptable path of 'achievement'.

There's nothing wrong with achievement, of course. And for some people, this path *does* bring personal fulfilment. Perhaps you do get the job and the partner and the promotion, and in the end you feel satisfied. When it comes to shaping your life, there are countless ways to design it – and if you stumbled straight into depth, purpose and meaning, that's great. I hope the tools in this book can be an addition to your lifestyle. For the rest of us, our paths might have taken a different direction.

Some of us realized the futility of chasing success early on and switched into another way of life altogether. Some of us continued the chase, progressing towards targets that always felt just out of reach. And some of us reached the targets or goals we'd set for ourselves and found that they didn't deliver whatever it was we'd expected from them.

There are a few consistent factors here that we'll return to throughout the book. One is the subjectivity of success: the realization that other people's ideas of a good life don't necessarily match our own. Another is the evolution, between generations, of what 'success' looks like. In many cases, ideas of traditional career paths have been replaced with a more personal, individualized range of options. For the next generation of leaders, it's increasingly possible to craft a fulfilling career without trudging through layers of corporate hierarchy. Job descriptions might be more malleable; portfolio careers are open to be designed, and sharing parts of yourself – your life, your story, your content – can be done without the backing of a traditional media outlet. And, relatedly, our growing awareness of *all* the options out there, appearing in front of us every time we open social media, can give us the confidence and security we need to question whether pre-existing ideas of success are *actually* working for us. All of this, potentially, leading us to the realization that what we've been working towards, the whole time, hasn't even been something *personally* meaningful to us.

4. A GLOBAL PANDEMIC, AND WHAT COMES NEXT

Finally, to wrap up this section, we should consider the most important contextual factor of the last few years. It would be difficult to find an industry, sector or individual that wasn't affected by the pandemic, each in entirely unique and diverse ways. The shifts in society – the ways we live, work and encounter each other – are huge, of course. But in this book, we'll touch mainly on the elements relevant to the existential experience we have, as individuals, in our own lives. In this respect, one of the most interesting aspects is the opportunity for reinvention and reflection. For many of us, a period of isolation, however it was imposed on us, gave us a significant amount of time to reconsider habitual patterns and tendencies. Maybe we noticed a reliance on certain distractions or coping mechanisms, or we started to re-evaluate behaviours we'd been carrying out for years, unnoticed. Periods of social and personal recalibration don't often collide in such an obvious way, and – as we steadily emerged from periods of lockdown – many of us wanted a *new* version of how things used to be.

Another element of post-pandemic life is a clearer understanding of what really matters. This includes things as complex as the reconstruction of economic policy – for example, more investment in healthcare or a reassessment of working environments – or things as individual as a personal decision to spend more time with loved ones. Some of us decided we needed to move out of cities. Some of us decided we needed a new career or a new relationship. Some of us decided to craft a whole new identity, one based around a sense of personal values and purpose. None of this was the priority in getting through the pandemic, of course – personal development can generally take a back seat in times where our lives and health are on the line. But once we moved through the pandemic years, many of us ended up with a clearer sense of what *really* matters. The job you thought formed part of your identity? Maybe you realized it was only a tiny part of who you are, on a personal level. That group of people you used to socialize with every weekend? Perhaps you haven't heard from them in months. The fast-paced lifestyle you couldn't see yourself ever leaving behind? It might feel less crucial these days; less integral to the way you move through the world; less *part of you*, and more something that you chose, at a particular point in time. The patterns we create in life are changeable, impermanent and adaptable to the evolving nature of things around us.

A last point, in the context of the pandemic and everything that it brought along with it: we have a sense, now – collectively as well as individually – that change is coming. There's a growing understanding now, and especially among the next generation of leaders and thinkers, that things *can't* go back to the way they were. We live in a fractured world, and one that we seem to be committed to destroying in a variety of ways. Climate change, racial injustice, a lack of social mobility, persistent inequality, the polarization of politics – the list is lengthy, and this barely touches the surface. But with change comes opportunity. The opportunity to see things differently. To start with ourselves, and then work outwards, to our relationships and communities and our work in the world.

So, what next?

This book advocates for a personal sense of depth and meaning *first*, but, ultimately, this work is intended to go beyond the self. As we move through the exercises in the book, the opportunity is not just to reform or refine or 'perfect' the self, but to extend this work outwards: to make the changes you want to see in the world, and to do it on behalf of other people as well as for yourself. This shift in perspective is one of the elements that distinguishes the methodology in this book from traditional self-help. Of course, the intention is to help *you*, the reader. But the ultimate, underlying purpose is to send this work back into the world, to re-enter your life as a whole, integrated, fully *alive* person, and then to use this as your foundation to make your own contribution. Nothing is isolated, or separate, or detached. Everything you do matters – and, most importantly, for the context of this book, *who you are* matters. It matters not just for you but for everyone you encounter, and, ultimately, for all of us.

CHAPTER 2

The Architecture of Your Life

● ● ●

In this chapter, we'll dive into the principles of this book and how they compare to other approaches. We'll take a quick look at the self-help industry, the traditions and teachings behind our work together, and a few overarching ideas that will start to emerge. Along the way, we'll begin to lay the foundations for the path ahead.

You, the storyteller

How far do you like to plan ahead? Do you know what you want to be doing in five years' time? How about one year? Six months? Next weekend?

Sometimes we're encouraged to look ahead. Our bosses want us to make career plans. Our friends want us to agree on social commitments. Our parents want to know when we're settling down, or moving out, or getting our lives together. This ability – to look to the future and speculatively map out our lives – is, perhaps, a uniquely human skill. We're story-tellers, by nature, and the act of imagining and committing to an unknown future is another application of this talent. We imagine what *might* happen, and we plan for that. And as much as this is about storytelling, it's also about taking authority – about standing in the position of creator, when it comes to your life. Deciding how you want things to look; taking steps to get there.

To begin, let's look at things on a smaller, more immediate scale. Imagine something unexpected happens to you. Perhaps you marry the person of your dreams and the relationship breaks down. Or someone you love becomes ill and you give up your career to take care of them. Or perhaps you work for a decade to get your dream job and suddenly the market crashes and the job opportunity goes away. There are a million ways our lives can fall apart, some big, some small. But life's unexpected changes can also come as a result of *good* things happening. Perhaps you get a promotion and end up moving abroad. Or you fall in love and reshape your life according to new, shared dreams. Or you find a new skill, passion or interest that takes your life in a different direction.

The consistent theme here, between all the good and the bad things, is the unexpected, unpredicted nature of all the possibilities that can happen. The skill we're developing in this book is not the ability to 'plan' your life. There are a million books out there to help you with goal-setting, vision-building, productivity, strategy and execution. This book is about something different. Instead of looking at our surface-level responses to the things that can happen to us – a change of job, a new relationship – we're going deeper. We're looking at the fundamental attitude you hold with regards to the things that come your way. We're going all the way down, into your core beliefs about yourself and your life and your everyday existence.

The journey ahead of us

For this work, we'll be moving across a range of disciplines and fields of study. We'll look at logotherapy, the therapeutic approach designed to navigate topics of meaning and purpose. We'll take a quick look at traditional monastic practices and see what we can learn from immersive, committed spiritual disciplines. And we'll touch on a few other paths to finding meaning, purpose and self-awareness, including meditation, contemplation, creativity, philosophy and embodied practices.

To be clear, before we dive in: I don't believe there's a single answer to the 'big' questions of life. Following the billions of human beings who have passed through this world, asking themselves the same things about life and meaning and happiness, it would be a little surprising to suggest there is, in fact, a simple, straightforward answer that applies to everyone. Instead, I want to offer you a few approaches that you might not have encountered before. These are the findings from my own meaning-seeking journey over the last decade, and I'd love to share with you the pieces of practical wisdom I've collected. And to be clear, none of these paths *alone* has delivered me a perfect sense of clarity about who I am or how to live. Instead, I'm advocating for an integrated approach – learning as much as you can, gathering wisdom from wherever you find it, and drawing it into your own life in a way that feels authentic. This is a way in which you can begin to craft a life – a life that belongs fully to you, and one that responds to all of your different preferences and characteristics, and to your ever-evolving sense of what it means to be fully alive.

This book is full of tools, techniques and pieces of advice for you to take out into the world and try for yourself. There's no overnight solution: a lifetime is barely long enough to really explore these questions. But I think one of the greatest gifts of this work is its infinite nature. There's no finish line, no completion date. Even if you do encounter moments of realization and deepening, as I hope you will, there's still work to do on the other side. There's still a life to build and a path to keep walking.

In fact, it's partly the 'accomplishment' perspective that holds us back from really leaning into the process, and – perhaps – even enjoying the journey. Maybe this perspective comes from the dominant cultural narrative – an *achievement culture*, where work is done to be demonstrated, or held up for approval, or posted about on social media. We've all encountered the humble-bragging posts of LinkedIn or the impossibly perfect images of Instagram. Meanwhile, there's not much appreciation for the quiet, imperceptible work that goes into building a life. This work is often messy, difficult, chaotic, draining and seemingly pointless. The results might be decades away. The 'reward' might be totally invisible. A better sense of self-awareness, or a feeling of being 'fully alive' – these aren't things that lend themselves to certificates or awards ceremonies. And yet, as we'll see, this work filters out. It starts in the innermost parts of the self, and it spreads out to touch every aspect of your life. Equipped with a better sense of being here in the world, of belonging, of knowing yourself, of experiencing life *fully*, you give yourself a secure foundation from which to do anything else – career success, relationship stability, financial goals ... and yes, even an attractive social media profile. If you want.

A few things about self-help books

The self-help genre is subject to a good deal of criticism. Here's the general objection: it encourages a cycle in which you, the reader, buy a book, hope it will change your life, it doesn't, you add it to your bookshelf and go looking for the next one, and the cycle starts again. And it's a fair point. If a book – or any other product, for that matter – promises a quick journey towards a better existence, there's reason to be hesitant.

You might have discovered this book in the 'self-help' category, but the work in this book has an alternative intention. Here are a couple of ways in which we'll be taking a different journey.

Self-help is usually about an outcome

For a start, this book is not promising you any specific result: in other words, we're focusing much more on process rather than outcome. At the end of this book, and even after doing the work for a number of years (or decades), you might not have a new job, or a new set of social skills, or a new body, or a new partner. This book is not about achievement, it's about experience. And many of the practices in this book come from traditions that don't believe in one-time solutions. Take monastic life, for example – this is a clear illustration of a lifestyle that doesn't have a defined outcome. You don't 'graduate' from monasticism. You just keep your ultimate purpose in mind and then continue on the path every single day, typically for the rest of your life. When it comes to the material in this book, there are some similarities with the monastic path. You're steadily changing your everyday experience of the world, gradually exploring life a little deeper than you did before. It might mean you stay in the same relationship but experience it in a different way – more present, more aware, more attentive, more joyful. You might stay in the same job but understand your purpose a little more. You might be living in the same house, or in the same town, or on the same budget, but with more appreciation, more wonder, more *life* than you had before.

Self-help usually starts from the outside

While most self-help books focus on the outer layers of the self ('how to look great and be wealthy, with glowing skin'), this one starts in a different place. We're not working on the most visible parts first. This, in a society that praises beauty, youth and aesthetic perfection, can seem almost counterintuitive. Isn't that the point, to have the perfect body, the perfect image, the perfect house? Isn't that where happiness actually is?

Well – it might be, for some people. As we explored earlier, there's no 'one-size-fits-all' to the biggest questions of life. And to be sure, the path we're starting in this book presents countless challenges: it requires us to really engage with the intricacies of our lives, and to stay committed to the task over a long period of time. It's certainly more straightforward to map out your skincare routine than it is to map out the architecture of your existence. But in this book, we're starting right at the heart of everything, diving in with insights and traditions and teachings that go to *who you are* and *how you live*, and then we'll work out from there. (Who knows, this might actually be the secret to glowing skin after all.)

Self-help books often go broad. This one goes deep

Instead of going broad, covering a topic or subject with multiple strategies and tools, we're going deep, focusing on just one central aspect: how to feel more fully 'alive'. In the process, you can expect many more questions than answers. We're looking at the problem from many different angles, examining it and stepping back from it, and then returning to look at it through different lenses. And in the end, we're not expecting to have a perfect 360-degree image of a solution, but a real-life experience of encountering the questions – and, ultimately, encountering yourself.

Self-help books tend to instruct. This one lets you lead

When it comes to something as intimate and personal as your life, it's pretty unlikely that you'll find one ultimate guide or a single teacher to show you the way. This is a good thing, in most cases. You want to be in the driving seat for the choices you make, especially those that relate to the way you experience the world. So, while a lot of self-help books take an instructional approach – which may well work in those contexts – this one lets you lead the way. The experience of being alive (and being curious about that experience) is mostly a process of figuring out, *for yourself*, exactly what works and what doesn't. It's less about being told and more about experimenting, discovering and curating a portfolio of practices for yourself.

Self-help books take you to the end. This one just starts the engine and hands you the keys

By the conclusion of most self-help books, you'll feel like you reached the end. A method has been outlined, or a set of steps has been planned out, and you're ready to finish. But with the work in this book, we're just beginning the journey – once we reach the end, the rest of the path is up to you.

A few recurring principles

This book works through four major sections: Mind, Body, Work and Self. Within those categories, we'll cover the various fields of study that have something to teach us – existential therapy, monasticism, meditation, philosophy and much more. But before we get started on the journey, there are a couple of general principles that will accompany us along the way. You'll see these principles arising in various contexts and in various forms – and as much as I believe in honouring each discipline with its own discussion, it's helpful to see the over-arching themes and ideas that can be identified. We'll talk a little more about bringing it all together in the final chapter – that is, the idea of *integrating* these ideas into the context of your everyday life – but for now, let's explore a few main principles.

PRINCIPLE 1: PRACTISING LIFE AS A DISCIPLINE

See if you can bring to mind the most generous person in your life. Visualize their face. Try to recall a few examples of their generosity. Now do the same, but for the quality of kindness. Again, bring that specific person to mind (perhaps it's the same person, or someone else). Recall a few instances of their kindness, demonstrated through their actions or intentions, that made you immediately associate them with this quality. And finally, do the same exercise, but for happiness. Think of the most joyful, happy person you know – someone who seems to have an enduring sense of happiness throughout all the challenges of life. Someone who stands out as radiating something *different*, something joyful.

The chances are, with regards to the three people that you have in mind, you've allocated them a certain identity. If they came up in conversation, you'd assume certain things about them: that they're a particular type of person, or that they're likely to react to a situation in a particular type of way. We often think of these characteristics as inherent abilities. Perhaps we say that they've 'always been like that', or that they're just 'that type of person'. This may be true, to some extent – there are certainly people who are predisposed to certain types of behaviour. But there's another perspective, and this is to see these personal qualities as elements that can be learned or practised. This is the discipline of building the self, intentionally, step by step.

This might seem strange at first, because we often don't think of these types of personal characteristics as things to be practised. I'm sure we could both think of a handful of books on developing social skills, or on public speaking, or on professional development. It's more challenging to think of a book on developing empathy, or compassion, or gratitude (at least, without going into the realm of spirituality or religion). Of course, there are books that help you develop certain character aspects – such as self-confidence – that might have compassion, joy or generosity as a side-effect. But, in general, it's as if we think we can more easily develop ourselves into excellent professionals, productive workers or impressive public speakers, but other elements of our character might be fixed in place from the beginning. We assume that some people are just 'the type' to be kind, generous, compassionate, joyful, optimistic (or fill in the gap with another description here).

The practices outlined in this book take a different approach. Though the exercises themselves come from different schools of thought, or from different traditions and backgrounds, they share a belief in the fluidity of the human experience. We'll learn, through the exercises and challenges contained in the chapters, that our personalities are not set in stone, that our lives are not on a fixed course, and that we're ultimately creative beings, with the ability to redefine our responses to anything that happens to us. We'll see this in the field of existential psychotherapy, as we approach our lives from a position of authority and freedom of choice. We'll see it in the monastic tradition, as we cover practices designed to realign our lifestyles in accordance with a clear purpose. And we'll see it again in the practices of meditation and mindfulness, as we take a look at the ability to observe our thoughts, and to be an aware, awake participant in our lives. Each of these practices brings countless unique aspects with it, as well as an entirely separate tradition and heritage. But they share the belief in the importance of our lives, and of us – as a main character in our life's story – as carrying the ability to shape our own narrative.

PRINCIPLE 2: THE LONG, LONG ROAD

How long is your attention span? Are you really focused on reading (or listening) to this sentence, or are you multitasking? Are you thinking about something else? Skipping ahead to the next paragraph?

Research indicates that our attention span is rapidly decreasing. In 2000, it was 12 seconds. In 2015, it was just above eight seconds.[1] And now, as you're reading this (assuming you haven't been distracted elsewhere), it could be even less. We live in a world that caters to restlessness: we might be sitting still, but we're travelling at a hundred miles an hour. To get our attention, things have to promise us speed – we want to know when the results are coming and how soon we can start to see them. Sure, this might make for an effective marketing strategy. But we lose something in the process: an appreciation of slow movement, of careful intentionality and of long-term creation.

Whatever we cover in this book, we're taking a long-term view, diving into the material as a practice or as a discipline. We're thinking about a shift in mindset, not to achieve a certain result or attain a certain aesthetic but to realign our everyday awareness and experience of the world. This work takes time, and it might even be a while before people around you notice that you're doing this type of 'depth'-focused work in your own life. That's OK: this work isn't designed to impress anyone else. This is for you – for your life, and for your participation in the world.

One of the most challenging aspects of this work is that you can't really *see* anything happening – or, at least, not straight away. In most cases, a satisfying element of personal transformation is the moment you spot the first signs of change – perhaps you've been slowly adding funds to a savings account, or gradually decluttering your house, or working on a new fitness regime. There's a reason we love the 'before and after' images of change – it's exciting to see how visibly different things can become, if you put the effort in. It's also a good way to keep yourself motivated – you notice the external change and it gives you the fuel to keep going. But the work we'll do in this book is different, and it will require a different set of skills to stay motivated and focused.

A good example of this concept is found in the practice of meditation. If you imagine someone who meditates, compared to someone who doesn't meditate, you probably make some immediate assumptions. On one hand, you might imagine the person who doesn't meditate to be irritable, quick to anger, impulsive. They're always in a rush, for some reason. They probably get annoyed at other drivers when they're stuck in traffic. And you might imagine the person who meditates to be the opposite. They float through life on a little cloud of enlightenment. They accept all of life's challenges with a quiet smile. They're never rushing – and they certainly don't get annoyed in traffic.

These two contrasting images (of the *external* impact of a practice like meditation) are unhelpful, because inner practices can't always be measured by their outward manifestation. While there is a good amount of research to suggest that meditation changes the neurochemistry of the brain,[2] it doesn't necessarily follow that a few months of meditation will instantly change the way you appear to other people (or the way you react in traffic, for that matter). There *are* eventual external changes that result from these practices – that much is clear. But it's not a linear process with guaranteed results. After a decade of practising various forms of meditation, I can tell you that – yes – I am more calm, less rushed, less anxious. But I'm also still working on all of these things, and these are disciplines that I'll be integrating into my life for years to come. (And I can't guarantee I don't still get annoyed in traffic.)

PRINCIPLE 3: GLIMPSES OF THE ANSWERS

There's an old parable about an elephant, originating from an Indian folk tale, that sums up this third principle well. In the parable, three blind men live in a small village. None of these men had ever encountered an elephant before, although they'd heard about them in stories. One day, the men were invited to enter the king's palace and visit an elephant that was kept there. The men surrounded the elephant and reached out to touch it. The first man touched the side of the animal and felt the scope of the elephant's body. To him, he declared, it felt like a wall. The second man touched the trunk. To him, he announced, it felt like a giant snake. The third man tugged on the tail. He mocked the other two men – to him, the animal just felt like a piece of old rope. The three men, unable to see the totality of the animal, were simultaneously correct and incorrect.

What we're looking at, in this book, is the (metaphorical) elephant of your existence. Your existential elephant is a complex thing, made of up interconnecting parts and elements, and incorporating all of your experiences and preferences and unique thoughts and feelings. All of it has a particular place in making you who you are, and in providing you the opportunity to design your life. But, in our journey together, we're walking round the elephant, slowly, figuring it out piece by piece. It's difficult to ever see the whole thing from every angle, but we'll gradually get to know each of the different aspects. At times, it seems unfamiliar – a daunting task. At times, we think we have it figured out – isn't the elephant just a piece of rope, really? And at times, as the bigger picture eventually forms, we can easily get overwhelmed. I don't think these responses are negative – just pieces of the journey. (This is the process of diving into your existence, after all. Maybe it would be more surprising if you *weren't* a little overwhelmed.)

PRINCIPLE 4: LIFE AS A PORTFOLIO

The word 'portfolio' is developed from an Italian word *portafoglio*, generally translated as a 'case for carrying loose papers'. The imagery is helpful when it comes to our existential work: we'll move through a couple of different schools of thought and practice, and we'll be gathering as we go – making notes, trying things out, experimenting with our own lives. We'll be taking things from different disciplines and putting them into our portfolio, to end up with something that is uniquely designed for us and meets us where we are.

The portfolio concept is also helpful because a portfolio is a fixed holder for moving pieces. In this analogy, the portfolio – when it comes to the work of this book – is your life: the context and background and experience and relationships that you bring to the pages of this book. It's the family structure you were born into, and your education and work background, and the places you spend time in. Into that portfolio you'll be adding and removing practices however you like. As we move through the meditation sections, those practices might form a part of your portfolio, for a period of time. And, at some point, as your life evolves, you might swap them out for something else – existential therapy exercises, for example, or another creative practice. So, the central point is not necessarily the practices themselves. The point is your intentional integration of the practices into your life, and the subsequent process of carefully observing whether or not they work for you.

It's certainly true that these practices don't *have* to take a portfolio approach. For those who are ready to dive head-first into a practice like meditation, mindfulness, Existential Analysis or another spiritual practice, this can be a truly fulfilling path. Many of these practices carry backgrounds and traditions that bring with them a full-life commitment (something like monasticism was never intended to be dipped in and out of, for example). But this – the dipping in and out idea – is not the intention of this book. Instead, think of the book as an introduction – to practices you may not have otherwise encountered, and to valuable lessons that are both contained within, and transcend beyond, the areas we'll cover. For those who find a natural affiliation to a certain lifestyle or type of practice – by all means, jump right in. And for those who prefer the portfolio approach, that's an option too. The only thing we're looking for, in this context, is a deepening of your personal experience of being alive. So long as you're honest with yourself about where and how you find that, and so long as you're pursuing a path that feels authentically aligned with who *you* are, then the choice is yours.

PRINCIPLE 5: THE THING ABOUT GIVING BACK

There's an exercise that I use often with clients in the context of existential work[3]. The exercise is called the 'five why' method, and you can do it with yourself, to get to the heart of many deep questions you're working on. The 'five why' method is pretty simple. You start with a statement, perhaps about what your purpose is. And then you ask, *why*? You give an answer. And then you ask, *why?* You repeat that process five times, until you get to the final answer, at the heart of all of your 'whys'. (I sometimes refer to this final answer as the 'foundational why'.)

If you played out the exercise with a career-related question, it could go a little like this:

I want to study medicine.
Why?
Because I want to become a doctor.
Why?
Because that's my dream career.
Why?
Because I want to help others.
Why?
Because it's important to me.
Why?
Because helping others in this way gives me a sense of meaning.

This is a generalized example, and, of course, you won't always end the exercise by unveiling some grand mission about changing the world. But what I have noticed, from working with this exercise hundreds of times, is that *very often* the exercise ends with some kind of 'giving back' element. In fact, at the heart of most people's mission, drive, vision, goals and dreams, there's often an element of giving something back. It doesn't have to be a global ambition. It doesn't even have to be an ambition that helps *everyone*. But, far more often than not, I hear people say over and over again that they want to make some kind of change to benefit others. This – in any form it arrives in – is the principle of 'service', and we'll be diving into it much more in the coming chapters.

It's been interesting to me, in my journey through various fields of thought and practice, to see the consistent focus on helping others, a theme that seems to keep coming up. I saw it in monasticism, with the focus on serving and being in community. I saw it again in meditation and mindfulness, with the practices of loving-kindness and generosity towards others. And I saw it in existential psychotherapy, where a person's core 'purpose' or 'meaning' in life is so often wrapped up with other people.

One interesting aspect of this theme, as we'll see throughout the book, is that it actually releases a lot of pressure on you, the reader (or listener), to craft a perfect life for yourself. We live in a world that *loves* to praise the individual, often over and above the community. Most of the books we read about self-help are precisely that: 'help' to improve and develop the 'self'. But part of this work goes deeper – not just analysing the self, but focusing on all of the connections that we have with other people, and with the world in general. We'll be navigating the different layers of our experience, looking not only at how to make *ourselves* better, but on what we want to create with our lives. On how we want to contribute to the world. On those we want to make an impact on, and how we want to help them. This work tends to unfold naturally, so don't worry too much about quickly crafting big visions of service and benevolence. To begin with, it's just a subtle perspective shift – from the idolization of the self, to the celebration of the self in support of others, and – more broadly – in support of the world we share.

CHAPTER 3

The Creator Methodology

● ● ●

Before moving into the four main categories (Mind, Body, Work and Self), this chapter covers the methodologies that underlie the practices in this book. We'll explore a couple of central tools to support the work ahead, including the 'design' mindset, existential autonomy(!), creativity and artistic life design, and much more.

Welcome to your life

Imagine you were given a brand-new life. In this brand-new life, you're allowed to be whatever kind of person you want to be. You can redesign your entire character, bringing in the qualities and characteristics you love and setting aside the ones you don't. What kind of identity would you create? Who would you look to for inspiration? Is there anything you'd want to leave behind?

Many people see the world as a fixed reality: we are who we already are. Our personalities are established. Our choices – both past and future – seem inevitable. According to this fixed perspective, the world throws stuff in our direction and we do our best to battle on. This is a tempting way to approach our lives because it absolves us of any responsibility for intentionally crafting our own paths. If the world is fixed, then we don't have to bother thinking about any of this. And when it comes to answering the question, 'So, what's the point of it all?' – well, that's just *the way life is*.

But there's a different way to approach your life. At the heart of this different perspective is the idea that you – yes, you, reading this right now – are the author of your own experience. You are, in fact, the creator of your identity. That brand-new life we imagined just a few paragraphs ago? That's closer to reality than it might have sounded. The new identity you thought about? That's actually available to you right now, in any given moment.

All of this sounds suspiciously like an Instagram ad ('Manifest your first million by the end of the week!'), but it's a perspective that's been around for thousands of years. It shows up in spirituality, literature, meditation, art, philosophy – and much more. Throughout this chapter, we'll be looking at this 'creator mindset' through a couple of different perspectives, but let's start with one particular approach to the idea: the field of existential therapy.

Exploring existence

At the heart of the modern existential therapy movement lies the work of Viktor Frankl. If you recognize the name, there's a good chance you've picked up a copy of *Man's Search for Meaning*, Frankl's classic text that sold (at last estimate) over 10 million copies. The first half of the book recounts Frankl's experiences as a prisoner in a Nazi concentration camp – the transcendence of love and purpose; the fight against despair; the power of the human spirit. What is often remembered in less detail, however, are the ideas of psychotherapy that are introduced in the second half of the book. Frankl's approach was termed 'logotherapy' and was developed not only as a psychotherapy for those needing therapeutic intervention but also as a *preventative* measure. The ideas within logotherapy were intended to help those who were dissatisfied with a fixed perspective of life; those who demanded more depth and meaning and responsibility; those who wanted more from life and were willing (or could be assisted) to go looking for it.

There are a few core principles at the heart of logotherapy: first, that life can have meaning in all circumstances, even the worst circumstances imaginable; second, that we have the *freedom* to find meaning for ourselves in any given situation; and third, that the search for meaning is central to human existence. Frankl's own life is an extraordinary exploration of these principles in action, so let's start there.

Frankl, as a prisoner in a concentration camp, experienced some of the worst conditions imaginable. Taken from society, with his life's work erased, and losing nearly every family member, Frankl found himself surrounded by despair, death and destruction. It might seem to be the ideal conditions for loss of meaning – a sense of hopelessness, a lack of control, a loss of purpose. But, as it turns out, that isn't necessarily the case.

Instead of a loss of meaning, Frankl used his experience to craft a new perspective. Instead of asking, 'Why did this happen?', Frankl turned *towards* the suffering, utilizing its transformative power. In this approach, the way in which we choose to bear our suffering can provide another source of freedom within our lives. Frankl viewed life as an *opportunity* to create, not as an existing state to be accepted. It's the creative power at the heart of logotherapy that forms the foundation of this book – and we'll return to these ideas in more detail later.

Hopes, dreams and disappointments

OK, back to you. As much as we can hold others up as a striking example, things can get a little more difficult when it comes down to our own daily lives. When the worst things come our way – grief, loss, change, heartbreak, illness – it can be difficult to maintain the perspective of opportunity and self-creation. Sometimes the last thing we want to do in those situations is make something 'new' out of it. In many cases, it seems easier to sit with the disappointment and despair. It certainly requires less energy to allow life to come 'at' you, instead of trying to shape and form it for yourself. But to think of this methodology as if it were 'making the best of a bad situation' is a misunderstanding. We're not trying to sugar-coat reality or ignore the facts in favour of adopting a positive attitude. We're talking about something far more interesting than that.

What we're talking about, here, could be referred to as a 'position to life'. We started this chapter with an example of a fixed perspective: surrendering to the things that come your way, and taking no responsibility for turning them into something meaningful. Logotherapy and Existential Analysis offer a different perspective. Viktor Frankl refers to this as a 'yes to life': an assertion of authority over your existence. It doesn't mean rejoicing at everything that comes your way, or glorifying the suffering that life might bring. But what it *does* mean is taking an open position: accepting responsibility for authoring your own life, and choosing your response to the situations you find yourself in. When it comes to suffering, then, it's not about simply accepting it, on the one hand, or powering through with positivity, on the other. It's about standing in a position of choice, deciding to *create* something new from whatever you've been given. This switch in positions is much deeper (and more meaningful) than emotional reactions or superficial responses. According to logotherapy, this is living at the 'highest' level.[1] One of the most interesting aspects of this field of psychology is that it doesn't just exist in a textbook or in a therapist's office. It can be lived out in reality.

An approach from meditation

If you've encountered practices like meditation or mindfulness, some of this might be starting to sound a little familiar. In my experience as a yoga and meditation teacher, I've seen similar concepts – of autonomy over our own experience – show up across Buddhist philosophy and in modern versions of mindfulness practice. A simple example of this is a seated meditation practice, where the intention is to focus on your breath. As thoughts come into your mind, you observe them, acknowledge them and then let them pass. Part of the beauty of the practice is in its simplicity (which, of course, doesn't mean it comes easily). What you're training the mind to do, in essence, is to create a *gap* between thought and response. A thought comes into your mind; you observe; you pause; you choose what to do next.

Comparing this to the 'fixed' mindset that we covered at the start of this chapter, you might be able to see an alternative perspective emerging. Meditation is, of course, a practice – it's something that takes place at a certain time, with our full attention and awareness and focus. But its impact is much broader. Practising meditation consistently over a period of time enables the work to spill over into the rest of our lives. We start to adopt a different perspective to the things that come our way. We start to notice those 'gaps' between stimulus and response, so that – when the worst things happen to us – we see ourselves as possessing the authority to choose how to respond.

The similarities to the existential perspective are obvious, but worth repeating: these are positions to life that we're free to adopt, and they enable us to choose – to step into the position of creator (or observer), and to decide how we want to proceed.

You, the designer

There are a lot of 'life design' books out there – applying the ideas of design thinking to your own life. This book was not written by a designer (disclaimer: I can barely draw a stick figure), but there is something interesting at the core of this idea, and it links back to the topics we've already covered.

In this context, the principles of design thinking often include defining a problem, making a plan, prototyping and testing it, and redesigning or reinventing when the circumstances call for it – and we'll be covering some similar practical ideas in the course of this book. For now, though, let's go all the way back to the start, to see yourself as the designer, pen in your hand, looking at your life as a blank page. Stepping into the role of designer requires you to face the possibilities that lie ahead. It requires an openness to mistakes, failures and frequent realignment. It requires an awareness of the act of creation that is available to each of us, as we go about the process of crafting our lives.

We're surrounded by acts – and products – of creation. If you're sitting down, the chair you're sitting on is a product of creation. The room you're sitting in started with an act of creation. The same goes for the phone you'll probably check in a minute. These things didn't exist, at one point. And then someone (or, more likely, a lot of people) did the work of design and construction, and the thing(s) came into existence. Whether you're a designer, or an architect, or a software engineer, or a teacher, or a parent, or a writer, or a builder – we're all constantly creating. We do this on a daily basis, in the context of our work. It's less common, though, to take several steps back and look at our everyday lives – outside of the work context – as an opportunity for creative expression.

One final thought on design thinking. A designer is up against constraints: deadlines, limited resources, specifications, client expectations and so on. Our lives are like this, too: limited, in all sorts of ways, by our circumstances. Whether it's our education, our financial obligations or our responsibilities towards others, most of us are constrained in the ways we can design and redesign our lives over time. But this, in itself, is a part of the design process. Stepping into the position of creator often means navigating boundaries and obstacles. Perhaps it's more appropriate to think of it as 'co-creation' – the act of creating something *within* the context of the things that already exist. And this, of course, gives us even more opportunity to think, observe and then choose how to respond.

Being creative

It's interesting to think about the associations we have around the word 'creativity'. I grew up in a family of 'creative people': my parents (both professional musicians) and my grandparents (trained actors, architects and artists). I did a fair amount of creative stuff growing up, too – music, drama, dance. But I always preferred structure and rules to unbridled improvisation. I liked the strictness of a discipline – something like ballet, for example – over the kind of wild freedom we often associate with creativity. (And, eventually, I ended up as a corporate tax lawyer, perhaps not the first profession that comes to mind when you imagine a 'creative type'.)

At some point along the path of education, careers and stable jobs, we're encouraged to pack up the concept of creativity and put it in a box. This box gets handed to a select group of people – the artists, the musicians, the dancers, the actors, the writers, the entrepreneurs. Perhaps those people went off to specialist schools or colleges, pursuing their creative talents as their choice of career. And the rest of us? Maybe we followed a more traditional path – law school, or apprenticeships, or academic study. Over time, creativity often becomes something we unpack only on certain occasions, as if it were only ever relevant in the context of a 'creative drawing workshop', from precisely 2pm to 4pm on a Sunday afternoon.

What's the point of these boundaries? According to the *Cambridge Dictionary*, the word *creativity* can be defined as the 'ability to produce original or unusual ideas'. And we're doing this all the time. Before we're even conscious of the process, we're constantly taking ideas and refining them and creating something new. Without even trying, we develop new interpretations and perspectives. We're creating and constructing the world without hesitation, each time we receive information and *make* something of it. Think of the last time you tried to explain a concept or an idea to someone else. Thousands of other people might have done the same thing, maybe even using the same words. But it's the act of filtering information through your unique worldview and perspective that brings in the element of creativity. Whatever you're saying or doing, you're the first person to say or do it *in your way*, seeing through your eyes, shaped by your experience and intentions.

The other thing that we're constantly creating, without hesitation, is our own identity. One reason that the transition from child to teenager (and then into adulthood) can feel so challenging is that we're doing the difficult work of constructing a new self. This is a separate self from our family and peers: it's an establishment of our own position in the world. During this time, ready-made, strong identities can seem extremely appealing – certain fashions or interests or music tastes might become all-consuming. These kinds of new identities enable us to step out of one thing (our childhood self) and into a new position (our new, redefined self). Stepping into an identity like this, though, tends to last only for a certain amount of time. Eventually, we're called again to face the individual, personal questions of life, questions about who we are and who we want to be in the world.

Perhaps society didn't always pay as much attention to this period of time – this existential reorientation between childhood and adulthood. In previous generations, it might have been possible to step directly from being a young person, under the authority of a family unit, to a young adult, responsible for upholding a new family unit. But over time, as lifespans have lengthened and the gap between child and adult has widened, we've opened up an opportunity for reinvention and self-discovery. This period, as difficult as it seems while we're going through it, is the beginning of a creative endeavour that can last for the rest of our lives. Defining who we are – our likes, dislikes, preferences, boundaries, personality traits, characteristics, style and mannerisms – is a fundamentally creative step. It's about bringing something new into existence, a new self, using all the same imagination and innovation and insight you'd need for any piece of creative work. And the opportunity isn't only available as we approach adulthood. We have a chance to recreate ourselves at any point, if we're willing to do it.

An informed curiosity

There's an unspoken rule that tends to kick in somewhere around your mid-twenties. The rule is this: you're generally supposed to know what you're doing. Or, more accurately, you're generally supposed to *look like* you know what you're doing. For most of us, there's a point at which wide-eyed curiosity and openness to the world seem to become less acceptable. I noticed this rule in action a few years into working in the corporate world. At some point, there was a general understanding that even if you came across something totally unknown, you were supposed to *appear* as if you knew how to handle it. This makes sense, of course, in the context of a professional career: you want to give the impression that you have things under control. A client probably doesn't want their work handled by someone who openly confesses they've never done anything like it before. But, in the process of professionalization, we lose something important: a valuable attitude of curiosity and openness to the world.

If you've seen a young child explore a new environment, you'll know exactly what this looks like. It's a fascination with the unknown; a desire to figure things out; a persistent journey to explore and discover more. When we get older, we can shy away from this process of exploration. We don't want to look stupid, basically. Curiosity can be uncomfortable because it puts us in a position of vulnerability. All that openness and enthusiasm can leave us unprotected against the harsh realities of life.

I think there's a middle ground here, one that we'll explore throughout the book. That middle ground is an 'informed' curiosity. It's about starting from a position of self-awareness (in other words, the experience and knowledge about the world we've built up to get to this point), but retaining that valuable sense of exploration and excitement. It's about placing ourselves in the position of a student, ready to receive new perspectives and information. And, importantly, it's about the willingness to change our minds about a topic, or to be re-educated on a topic we thought we'd mastered already.

This middle ground of 'informed curiosity' is closely related to creativity, but it also shows up in a variety of other places.

Think about the scientific method, for example. Some consistent features of this method include observation, measurement, experimentation, and the formulation, testing and modification of hypotheses. And the foundation for this process? An informed curiosity: building on a base of established knowledge, but remaining open-minded to whatever result the process might deliver.

Another example of this attitude is the Zen Buddhist concept of a 'beginner's mind' (often termed '*shoshin*'). This concept – of approaching things as a beginner, ready to learn and receive – is not limited to studying or meditation. Instead, this is *a position to life*, or a 'lifestyle practice'. In exploring things as if we were seeing them for the first time, we tend to appreciate every single detail (a similar process is reflected in the practice of mindfulness). And it also comes with a certain lightness. Steve Jobs once described the feeling, upon being fired from Apple, like this:

> *I didn't see it then, but it turned out that getting fired from Apple was the best thing that could have ever happened to me. The heaviness of being successful was replaced by the lightness of being a beginner again, less sure about everything. It freed me to enter into one of the most creative periods of my life.*[2]

All this comes with a cost, of course. The world is generally structured to reward people who appear to know what they're doing. In many ways, adopting a beginner's mind is a countercultural position. It involves risk, uncertainty, vulnerability, humility and the potential for failure. But it also presents an opportunity for new things to arise. For those with enough courage to pursue it, this perspective can form the foundation for a creative, meaningful life.

Privilege and responsibility

Doing the work of creating your life is difficult, and challenging, and demanding – but it's also a privilege. To even get to the position of 'life design', the starting point requires some degree of stability and security. One way of illustrating this point is through Abraham Maslow's hierarchy of needs.[3] The hierarchy of needs is a social psychology tool that demonstrates several layers of human need. It begins with the most fundamental elements: first, physiological needs (food, shelter, clothing, sleep); then, safety needs, including economic security; and next, social needs, like love, community or belonging. On top of this is self-esteem, and, finally, at the summit of the hierarchy, self-actualization. Most people think the hierarchy ends there, at self-actualization (in other words, the need to fulfil our potential, or the desire for personal growth). But Viktor Frankl, the psychiatrist we discussed earlier on in this chapter, was reported to have supported another layer. On top of self-actualization, he thought, should be *self-transcendence*. And Maslow did, in fact, support this layer within his own work, with the result being that the hierarchy is not limited to the question – 'what do I need to live?'. Instead, it also encompasses the question – 'what am I living *for*?'.[4]

Let's return to the privilege point, to look at it from another angle. For those of us who are fortunate enough to reach a position where we can think about 'redesigning' our lives, we'll most likely be building on a solid base of safety and stability in other areas of our lives. In other words, we'll often need to be fairly settled – in our living circumstances and basic human needs – before the questions of meaning and purpose take priority. (This is obviously not always the case, but the experience of the majority.) But acknowledging the privileged standpoint can lead to inertia, because it's not always obvious how we should respond to it. In other words, how can we *use* our position to contribute something back to the world? This, then, is where the idea of responsibility comes in.

By choosing to undertake this work – the work of redesigning our lives – we also choose to take responsibility for the way in which our lives unfold. In other words, once we make the decision to design our responses to things that come our way, we also have to face up to the intentional ways we move through the world. That is, it involves thinking with a wider perspective – considering the other people who cross our paths and acting accordingly. It involves crafting a life that's meaningful, not just for ourselves but as a contribution to the world we share with everyone else.

And, relatedly, we're called upon to give back in some way. If we reach a sense of deep meaning and purpose – that feeling of being 'fully alive' – through the work of redesigning our lives, we can slowly, steadily, show others how to do the same. One of the most important aspects of the work we'll encounter in this book is its practical nature: more than studying it, you can actually *live* it, if you choose to do so. Your lifestyle, carefully crafted and oriented towards a full, fulfilling existence, can become a quiet, unspoken inspiration for other people.

Life as a gift

As far as we know, we didn't elect to end up here. But through a miraculously unique set of circumstances, we *are* here, fully formed by forces outside of our control. And it's not inevitable that we should see our existence as a 'gift', either. War, violence, death, discrimination, inequity and inequality, environmental destruction – the list of life's negatives is long, and not obviously outweighed by the positives. And (at least for me) the solution doesn't lie in a kind of superficial positivity, or an Instagram-filtered reality, or an edited existence that doesn't acknowledge how difficult the world can be. Of course, it's more complex than that. At the same time, we can look right at the complexity of it all – face it head-on, with determination and grit, and then decide to *make something* out of it.

This chapter has covered several different aspects of what I call the 'creator mindset', but this one might be the most important concept yet. It's the art – or, perhaps, the discipline – of seeing your life as a gift. We didn't choose to end up here, but we *did* end up here, and we can choose to fully utilize the time we get to spend here. We can choose to look at all of the pain and suffering that surrounds us: not closing our eyes to it, but choosing to respond to it. And we can choose to see it as an opportunity to shape the kind of world we want to live in. By seeing our life as a gift in this way, we can move through our days with a deepened sense of purpose. It's not easy or particularly comfortable, and it's certainly a different approach to the pleasure-seeking impulses we're often encouraged to adopt, but it's an intentional, meaningful way of being in the world. And once again, it places the creative power back in our hands, as the designers of our own paths.

We'll get into the practicalities of exactly *how* to develop this approach across the next few chapters. But first, let's look again at the design aspect, this time from the 'portfolio' perspective.

Back to the portfolio idea

The word 'portfolio' is most often associated with the 'portfolio career'. The creator behind this term, Irish writer and philosopher Charles Handy, described it as 'exchanging full-time employment for independence' (he called the concept 'going portfolio'). In more recent years, the 'portfolio lifestyle' has come to represent a collection of interests, passions and projects – including, but not restricted to, a career. The portfolio idea is an important element of the 'creator mindset' we've been covering in this chapter because it provides a framework for bringing the principles together. By building a portfolio, you start from a position of design, with the authority to choose which aspects you'll bring into your portfolio and which you'll exclude. And then you can begin the difficult, rewarding process of curation – understanding your desires and passions, and crafting a life that corresponds to them.

The portfolio concept is especially appealing in the careers context, and particularly (though not exclusively) for the newest generation entering the workforce. It provides space for creativity, for experimentation and for exploration. In the context of our careers, it can enable a fuller extent of our own personalities to be displayed. If we wanted to, we could cultivate a whole range of different roles and responsibilities that addressed each aspect of who we are, and include them within our personal portfolio. And so, bringing the 'portfolio' concept into this chapter, as an element of the creator mindset, seems appropriate. While a portfolio lifestyle doesn't necessarily give you any insight into exactly *what* you should be spending your time doing (we'll come on to that later), it can provide the structure you need to figure it out.

An integrated life

And so, to draw it all together, the concept of *integration*. The word itself, integration, is from a Latin word meaning 'made whole', and it comes with connotations of fullness and depth. It's at the heart of the pursuit towards becoming more alive, because it provides the coherence and elegance that help us make sense of our experience. Integration is about bringing all of the scattered parts of our lives together, in one place, to make something *new*. Again, this is an inherently creative process: the act of taking existing elements of your life (passions, interests, personality traits, preferences) and blending them together to create a full, integrated life.

As we move into the main chapters of this book, through the concepts of Mind, Body, Work and Self (amongst other things), we'll be taking the principles of this chapter with us. Existential psychology, life design, creativity, curiosity, responsibility and privilege, the unexpected gift of existence, and your very own life portfolio – all of these elements will become your tools as you start to do the work of becoming more fully alive. And, of course, the art of integration – bringing it all together to create something entirely unique and personal to you. Equipped with these initial ideas, with a blank page in front of us, and with a beginner's mind, we're ready to get started.

PART II

The Practices

CHAPTER 4

Mind

● ● ●

There's no shortage of mental health books available in the world. Meditation, mindfulness, wellness, productivity – I'm sure a multitude of authors and titles comes to your mind. But in this chapter, we'll be taking a slightly different perspective, focusing on practices designed to help you feel more *alive*, and working with deeper themes of purpose and meaning. As well as the more reflective traditions of meditation and contemplation, we'll be exploring some practical suggestions from existential psychotherapy to help you define your values and principles, as well as explore what a meaningful life looks like for you.[1]

Before we begin

I had my first panic attack at 18, in the back of the lecture hall of a law faculty. I can remember the experience vividly – chest tightening, heart racing, hands shaking. The feeling of not being able to get enough air, of scanning the room for the exit. At the time, I put it down to stress or lack of sleep, thinking of it as an unusual experience that probably wouldn't happen again. It wasn't until a few years later (and after a few more of those unusual experiences) that I was able to find the language I needed to talk about it, and the tools I needed to move on from it.

Even just over the last few years, the cultural conversation on mental health has shifted dramatically. Back at university, I blamed myself for being so anxious: after all, I was the one who voluntarily put myself in such a stressful environment. Everyone else seemed to be coping *just fine*. And it was a privilege to be there. I already felt like I didn't really deserve it, so to allow myself to acknowledge the way I was feeling felt ... well – a little self-indulgent. But these days, talking openly about stress, overwhelm, burnout or anxiety is more accepted, and we're constantly supplied with information – in the media, in advertising, and through the global wellbeing industry – to help us with these experiences. With that in mind, then, this chapter isn't a medical recovery manual, and we won't cover specific mental health conditions. Instead, we'll work through a variety of practices that could help us form a firm foundation for our lives as we move forwards. And the tools we'll explore aren't only designed for a quiet, peaceful, responsibility-free life. These are tools for navigating the fullness of life, in all of its complexity and overwhelm and exhaustion. These are tools designed for the long term, helping you to build up a steady sense of your own mental landscape, enabling you to see shifts and changes over time, and to make your own decisions about how to respond. And these are the kinds of tools I now use in my own life, every day, to find a more consistent sense of feeling grounded, focused, and fully alive.

As well as panic attacks and high-adrenaline situations, we also face the low-energy seasons of life – burnout, exhaustion or even just a steady sense of meaninglessness.

The practices in this chapter are designed for those experiences, too. Our intention with this work is not to 'solve' a problem but to lay the groundwork for the road ahead; to develop a set of skills and abilities that might just come in useful during the more difficult periods of life. And so, as we move into the search for meaning, and through the mind-focused practices of contemplation and meditation, we'll be setting up the structures that will support us through the times when it feels hard to keep going. Seeing this work as a discipline, or as part of your 'self-care' routine – equally as important as sleeping well or staying hydrated – might just provide a more stable sense of direction, purpose and intention when everything else becomes clouded.

The search for meaning

How did you spend your days at 17? If you're anything like me, you might have been dividing your time between a social life and keeping up with whatever reality TV was popular at the time. Seventeen-year-old Viktor Frankl, however, was busy developing a comprehensive philosophical worldview, for which he would later become globally renowned. Frankl's psychology was heavily influenced by other existential thinkers – including the philosopher Søren Kierkegaard – and began to take its final form in the late 1930s. Writing in 1938, Frankl spoke of a method that dealt with the 'totality of the human being', a psychotherapy that 'saw behind' surface-level issues to deal with the individual as a complex, whole, spiritually seeking being.

Frankl's global bestseller, *Man's Search for Meaning*, sets out his psychotherapeutic method – but Frankl's ideas were forming long before the publication of this work. Frankl was a periodic correspondent of Sigmund Freud and a student of Alfred Adler's school, both prominent and established psychiatrists and psychotherapists in the Viennese academic tradition. Over time, Frankl's own philosophy moved away from his early teachers and in the direction of a more humanistic psychotherapy (a term which means, in essence, therapy that takes into account the *human* elements of the client, and the client's future, goals and purpose). Where Freud and Adler adopted a more analytical approach (mostly centred around uncovering a behaviour and finding its origins in the client's past), Frankl's approach was future-orientated. Frankl's aim was to enable the client to take responsibility for their own life, using the resilient power of the human spirit. The name of Frankl's own school of thought, *Logotherapy*, is derived from 'logos', a Greek word often translated as 'meaning', 'purpose' or 'reason' (and, although unrelated to Frankl's work, a word that also shows up in religious translations as 'Word of God').

Frankl's new ideas eventually resulted in his expulsion from Adler's school of psychotherapy, despite having been one of the youngest, most promising members. For those of us who have been shut off from communities, family or friends on the basis of things we believe, or for different ways of thinking, it's easy to imagine how challenging these years must have been for Frankl. Appropriately enough, though, Frankl's belief in his *own* purpose gave him the energy to keep going.

As Frankl's beliefs and philosophy shifted, so too did the world around him. In the 1940s, Frankl was deported to a concentration camp, along with his family, and shortly after completing his first book. Dedicated to his work, Frankl hid his manuscript in the lining of a coat, but – after being forced to trade his coat for an older one – it was lost. For over three years, Frankl suffered deprivations beyond what most of us could imagine. Losing his entire family – including his beloved wife – Frankl struggled to survive. Around him, he saw death, devastation, starvation, torture and a complete loss of meaning on the part of many of his fellow prisoners. In *Man's Search for Meaning*, Frankl writes about his approach to meaning and purpose, the fundamental importance of honouring the call to meaning, and the psychotherapeutic approach that supported him through the journey. On a more personal level, Frankl attributed his survival to three main elements: his relationship to his family, his relationship to his work, and his relationship to his own spirituality.

At this point, if you're similar to me, you might be wondering why this field of meaning-focused therapy isn't more widely known. As someone who was actively searching for meaning, purpose and direction, it took me a good couple of years to figure out there was a fully established school of thought (in the form of logotherapy) that was already offering structured answers to many of my questions. This may, of course, have just been because my own searching wasn't quite thorough enough (entirely possible), or because logotherapy and similar approaches are still fairly new to the field of psychotherapy (also possible[2]), or because therapy-focused solutions to existential questions seem like a last resort, instead of being openly available to everyone, at any time. Admittedly, it does seem quite extreme to be seeking out 'existential therapy' for the big questions of life. But we don't necessarily need to work long term with a therapist to benefit from some of the tools and techniques from this field. In fact, we can dive into a few of them right now, in this chapter.

Two final notes about this type of work and its various applications. First, it's important to remember that logotherapy doesn't take a critical, exclusionary approach to an individual's search for meaning (it's not the *only* way to look at these questions, of course). Instead, it offers an approach, guidance and a set of tools with which to navigate the path towards personal fulfilment.

The second point is that the field of existential psychotherapy, as with most schools of therapy, continues to develop and shift and evolve. Alongside logotherapy, there are other schools of 'Existential Analysis', humanistic therapies and person-orientated therapies – and, no doubt, more forms of this work will take shape over the coming decades. All this is to say: there are lots of different ways of looking at the questions of meaning, purpose and existence from a therapeutic perspective. Since we're dealing with the most fundamental questions of life, this is – frankly – both unsurprising and exciting.

Learning from Logotherapy[3]

Before we jump into our first exercise, let's run through the basic ideas we'll be working with, which draw on the foundations of Frankl's psychology. These are, of course, high-level summaries that take their basis from the principles of logotherapy: to explore these principles in depth, and using technical descriptions from their primary sources, you'll find a list of logotherapy resources at the back of this book[4] (centred around Frankl's work).

PRINCIPLE 1: LIFE CAN HAVE MEANING IN ALL CIRCUMSTANCES – EVEN IF THE CIRCUMSTANCES ARE CHALLENGING AND DIFFICULT

In his description of the concentration camps of Nazi Germany, Frankl recalls stories of people who found a sense of purpose within the camps. In Frankl's interpretation, the ability to find a sense of personal purpose was placed in the hands of the individual. As Friedrich Nietzsche wrote, 'Whoever has a why to live can bear almost any how.'5 And we deal with a multitude of 'hows' every single day. Despite our best efforts, life can be challenging, chaotic and often seemingly pointless. We try our best, but we get bored, or we make mistakes, or someone lets us down, or we get disappointed and disillusioned. You don't need to live through an extreme version of suffering to know that ordinary life can be tough. And acknowledging that there are worse forms of suffering out there is not an enduring solution, either. Yes, we can – and should – be grateful for our opportunities and abilities. But this doesn't give us a shortcut to finding our own sense of purpose. We still have to do the difficult, deep, challenging work of figuring out what our personal *why* actually is, and then begin to integrate it into our day-to-day existence.

PRINCIPLE 2: THE WILL TO FIND MEANING IS CENTRAL TO OUR EXPERIENCE AS HUMANS

A central element of logotherapy is the idea that humans are motivated by the will to find meaning. This means, when it comes to the clinical use of modern logotherapy, issues like addiction, depression or anxiety could be linked back to a loss of meaning, in some cases (although, it should be noted, Frankl himself did not address these issues). With a topic like addiction, this interpretation isn't dissimilar to approaches taken in recovery organizations like Twelve-Step programmes (which generally focus on the concept of a 'higher power'). At the heart of many of these addiction recovery programmes is the idea of finding something of meaning, something of value. (As with most of the areas explored in this book, you don't have to *fully* agree with this approach in order to find something useful, or interesting, about it.)

PRINCIPLE 3: EVERY HUMAN HOLDS THE FREEDOM TO FIND MEANING IN THE EVENTS, EXPERIENCES AND OUTCOMES THAT COME OUR WAY

At a basic level, we have the freedom to decide how to respond to the things that come our way. To take a very simple example, let's look at a classic stimulus–response scenario. Imagine waking up tomorrow morning and going about your normal routines. Let's imagine you're preparing for another day in a job you enjoy doing. But when you check your email, you're shocked to see that you've been fired. The company no longer needs your services and – due to budget cuts – you're out of a position. How would you respond? How do you feel right now, even just reading through the example? Nervous, or anxious? Fearful that this scenario might, one day, actually happen to you?

One more example. Imagine waking up tomorrow morning and checking your email again – but this time there's a different kind of surprise. An email informs you that you've won a huge sum of money, the kind of amount that will change your life forever. How would you be feeling now? Excited? Overwhelmed? Eager to share with friends and family?

One of the central ideas of logotherapy is that each situation presents you with a choice. In the moment between stimulus (receiving the email) and response (some kind of emotional reaction), you can find a gap (or, perhaps, you can train yourself to observe a gap). Then, within the gap, you have the ability to make up your mind about what happens next. The following quote (often attributed to Viktor Frankl, although its true origin most likely lies elsewhere[6]) sums up this approach well:

> 'Between stimulus and reaction, there is a space. In that space is our power to choose our response. In our response lies our growth and our freedom.'

PRINCIPLE 4: THE HUMAN BEING IS A *WHOLE*, MADE UP OF BODY (IN GREEK, *SOMA*), MIND (IN GREEK, *PSYCHE*) AND SPIRIT (IN GREEK, *NOÖS*)

One of the issues with other forms of therapy, according to logotherapy, is that modern attempts to 'heal' or treat our problems leave out a third aspect – the spiritual dimension. This isn't the kind of spirituality you might hear about on social media – horoscopes, star charts, tarot cards, manifestations (not to say any of those are necessarily bad, if they're working for you). Instead, logotherapy's spirituality is more about the capacity for *self-transcendence* – in other words, the uniquely human ability to conceptualize personal forms of meaning and purpose, stretching far into the future, and the capacity to transcend the current state of being we're in, right now. You exercise this capacity every single time you make a plan for 'future you'. (In fact, the 'glow up' trends we often see on social media are a possible example of this capacity for transcendence. When you map out an upgraded version of your current existence, you create the ability to move beyond the self as it exists in the present moment.)

Other features of this 'spiritual' dimension, according to logotherapy, include our abilities to fall in love, to exercise creativity, to devote ourselves to a faith or religion, to imagine or dream up possibilities, and to discover – or come closer to – our own selves. In this sense, creating your 'self', or crafting your own identity, is a spiritual act.

A final element of the 'spirit', in this context. If we move through life without tending to our spirit, we end up – using the principles of logotherapy – without full health. This is an interesting idea when it comes to modern wellness trends, because we're all familiar with how health *should* look, or how wellness should be performed for the public. Morning routines, green juices, exercise programmes – we know how to work towards the ideal state of 'being well'. But it doesn't really touch the spiritual level – the search for meaning and purpose that so many of us feel called to. It's a privilege to be aware of this, of course, because our awareness is the first step towards finding *whole* wellness, and towards a deeper experience of life. So, when we talk about *wholeness* here, it's not just about mind and body, but about the unity of mind, body and spirit.

PRINCIPLE 5: OUR SEARCH FOR MEANING MIGHT BE BLOCKED IN A VARIETY OF WAYS, INCLUDING OUR CHASING OF MATERIAL POSSESSIONS, WEALTH OR STATUS. WANTING TOO MANY 'GOOD' THINGS CAN FORM A BARRIER TO THE THINGS WE ACTUALLY NEED

Have you ever fallen in love with someone at a particular place, or in a particular city, and then visited the same place again once the relationship is over, or the person is no longer here?

This can be one of the most painful experiences, after the loss of a relationship or a person, because you're revisiting a place that once seemed to contain meaning, but without the meaningful element to it. We can end up feeling a strange form of grief when this happens, mixed up with nostalgia and a longing for something that no longer exists. Perhaps it feels empty, as though the place promised something it could never deliver. Perhaps you know this feeling – getting what you want, on the outside, but feeling inner emptiness, despair, self-doubt, exhaustion. According to logotherapy, these are the classic signs of a loss of meaning. Because, in fact, it's usually never a place, or a city, or any other material element, in the end. The source of meaning is much deeper than that.

EXERCISE 1

The meaning tracker

The goal of this exercise is simple: to identify the parts of your life that give you a sense of meaning. For this exercise, start by taking a sheet of paper and making a number of columns. The columns have the following headings: 'People', 'Places, 'Objects', 'Experiences', 'Hopes'.

To begin the exercise, start by filling out the columns with everything you can think of that gives you a sense of meaning, under each of the headings. You can write as fast or as slowly as you like, and in any format: bullet points, diagrams, one-word answers, drawings – whatever helps you get it down on paper.

For example, under '**People**', list your most meaningful relationships, friendships and connections. Don't worry too much about whether you think they *should* be your most meaningful relationships, friendships and connections. The exercise focuses on *you*, and your experiences, and not on what you (or anyone else) think your experiences should be.

Under '**Places**', list all the places that make you feel alive. Track back over the years to recall seasons and locations that remained in your memory. Include everything, no matter how small. What about the places where you went to school, or where you travelled abroad, or a particular house (or even room of a house) you loved? You can use the different times of year to remind you of places – are there memories of holidays or other celebrations that feel meaningful to you? Are there particular places where you feel safe? Or cities that just naturally feel like home?

Under '**Objects**', get creative. Include all the objects in your life that have – or have previously had – a sense of meaning for you. (Your iPhone still counts, if it provides you with meaningful connections and information.) Aside from your devices, think about particular items of clothing, or decorations, or photos, or jewellery, or other possessions you find important. Ask yourself: what would you save if your house was burning down and you had only one or two items to take with you? Instead of *practical*, think *meaningful*. Which objects do you look at to remind you who you are, or why you do the work you do?

Under '**Experiences**', track back through your memories to recall things you experienced that felt particularly meaningful. You can return to this work over a period of weeks (or months, or years!), so don't feel discouraged if only a few things come to mind. Memory can be an unreliable thing – at least for me, it takes a while to recall all the times I did something that felt especially meaningful, even though there are many. To begin with, track through the central markers of time – birthdays, celebrations, graduations, weddings, moving house, moving cities, reunions and so on. Include the sad, nostalgic, grief-filled moments as well as the happier ones. Meaning, as we'll be discovering, is by no means limited to the 'good' experiences of life. If we're going after depth, we have to jump in head-first and take it *all* – the good, the bad, the painful, the challenging, the euphoric: this is our experience of the world, and we're able to claim all of it.

And finally, under '**Hopes**', include all the meaningful things you want for the future. If you hope to start a family, or move to another city, or get a particular job, or become a particular person, include it here. This is where you can really exercise that 'spiritual', self-transcendent dimension: move beyond your present self to imagine the things in the future that might bring you a sense of meaning. It's OK to focus on material possessions to start with, but make sure you *also* tap into the meaning-focused reasons behind your pursuit of those things. So, for example, if it's a new job that you want, think about *why* it is that you want it and what kind of meaning (beyond a great salary and an impressive new LinkedIn title) it might hold for you.

Once you have a few things in each column, step away from the work for a while, but keep it somewhere nearby. As the days pass, add to it – when you remember something, or when you encounter something distinctly meaningful in your everyday life and want to document it. The list isn't a one-time record, it's an evolving tracker, and it can grow with you over time.

There are a few things you can learn from this exercise, although none will give you a single answer about the meaning of your own life.

First, you can start to build a more comprehensive picture of what it is that currently delivers a sense of meaning and purpose in your life. From the things you love to have around you, to the places you connect with and the people who support you, you should be starting to see a structure of meaning developing. Perhaps it even reveals to you the meaningful experiences you can find in your everyday life; meaning that was, in fact, present all along.

Second, you get a little clarity on the things that have given you meaning in the *past*, the things that *currently* give you meaning, and the things that you hope will deliver meaning in the *future*. If you can see an obvious disconnect here (for example, if your future meaning-focused column is completely unrelated to the things that have delivered meaning in the past), it might be an opportunity for re-evaluation, either of the past, or the present, or the future. Only you'll be able to decide whether that re-evaluation is necessary and, if so, what the outcome should be.

And finally, you can see, on paper, the multitude of meaning-delivering possibilities that already exist for you. Most – if not all – of us have felt a loss of meaning, at various times and in various ways. Exercises like this can support you during those times, building up a strong awareness of the diversity and richness of your everyday life. You can see, just from dividing up the categories and filling out each one in turn, the places to which you can turn for a better sense of meaning and purpose. And it can also support you to develop these categories – if you find, for example, that your 'meaningful objects' column is a little emptier than the others, you can go in search of things that deliver or represent a sense of meaning. We're meaning-seekers, after all – the option to develop sources of meaning (or enhance existing ones) is always in our hands.

EXERCISE 2

Your core values

What comes to mind when you think about having a set of core values? The idea of being a value-oriented person can seem a little outdated or old-fashioned. For me, values sound like something your grandparents would talk about: 'in the good old days, we had a stronger sense of values' (or something like that). But, in logotherapy, the term 'values' has a different association. As humans, we move through a world full of situations that require our judgement. We have to decide what the meaning is of each ordinary moment in our life. If we had to do this by ourselves, we'd barely have time to do anything else – but, fortunately, we can rely on the reactions, responses and interpretations of millions of other humans before us. In other words, other people have established meaningful responses to any given situation. In some logotherapy writings, these established responses are called 'values', and sometimes 'universal values', because they apply broadly.

Before we get too deep into terminology, let's think of some practical examples. In most situations, we have an established set of values that indicate how we should respond: for example, the values of our parents, or the values of our cultural background, or the values of our religion. These are established, secure values that have been set up before we arrived at the situation. The problem is, we can get into situations where these values conflict. For example, the values of our parents might conflict with the values of our religion, or the cultural values of the places we choose to live. In those situations, we have to choose which values to follow: an opportunity to create our own path. Or, we could take even more responsibility and craft a new set of values for ourselves. This second type of 'values' (the values that you craft for yourself) is the type we'll be looking at in this exercise.

Influenced by Viktor Frankl, values could be found in three different categories: first, *creative*, second, *experiential* and third, *attitudinal.* Let's break them down into sections, and then we'll work through an exercise to figure out how to claim these values for yourself – and what this all means when it comes to your experience of life.

- **Creative values** can include drawing, writing, painting, design, composition, construction or architecture.
- **Experiential values** can include falling in love, nature, culture, music, drama, poetry, reading, playing games or taking part in sports.
- **Attitudinal values** can include your beliefs, mindsets or worldviews: how you see the world, yourself and others.

Grab a sheet of paper and a pen and set a timer for around 20 minutes. In that time, work through each category of values and ask yourself one question: *What values do I have that fall into this category?* Don't feel limited to the lists above – include all creative, experiential and attitudinal values you have, and feel free to add any that don't fall within those categories on an extra list of your own.

When you finish the exercise, skim back over your findings. If you can see any common themes arising between the categories – great. Consistency or recurrence of values is a strong sign of integration, something we'll be returning to later. As you might be starting to observe, the idea of *wholeness* is a central theme of this book, and seeing the same values arise again and again can be a sign that you're developing (or uncovering) a deep, holistic understanding of the self. On the other hand, if you can't see commonalities between the categories, don't worry. The first time anyone does this exercise, the results are often scattered. As with everything else in this book, the values exercise is designed to be repeated again and again, over a long period of time, and you might see themes emerge over the coming weeks and months. And, as always, there's no perfect answer. You can't get it wrong (or right).

One final task for you to carry into the rest of your week. For the next few days, make it a habit to check back on your lists of values – perhaps at the start or the end of every day. If it's helpful, make them into a note on your phone that you can access easily. Your assignment is to observe *where* these values show up in your life, and *how* you honour or protect them when they do. For example, let's say that one of your 'attitudinal values' is courage. Include this in your list. Then, when you're faced with a situation in which you have a choice between courage and fear, observe your response and make a note of it. The intention is not necessarily to change your behaviour but simply to observe your responses and reactions to the circumstances of your life. And, over time, the intention is to bring your everyday experience of life closer to the values you've identified for yourself.

■ ▰▰▰▰▰▰▰▰▰▰▰▰▰▰▰▰ ■

Meditation and reflection

As a meditation teacher, I hear one piece of feedback from my students over and over again. Pause, and take a guess as to what it might be. If you're a student of meditation (or another similar practice), you might have even complained about it yourself – or, at the very least, had the same thought cross your mind. It's not about the difficulty of the exercises or the challenge of silence. It's not about the length of time required, or the disciplined demands of the practice, or the lack of immediate results. In fact, it's about something much more fundamental, something that reveals a lot about the way we think and feel about ourselves on an existential level.

Here's the phrase: *I'm terrible at meditation.*

This has always been quite amusing to me because – on one level – I completely relate to it. I often feel as though I've failed at things if I haven't lived up to my own expectations. I'm very familiar with the feeling of being *not quite good enough* to do something with excellence. But – speaking as a meditation teacher – it's not really possible to fail (or succeed) at meditation.[7] In fact, when it comes to meditation, or contemplation, or other similar practices, we're entering a completely different frame of mind altogether. This is the mindset of *non-duality*, a term derived from the Sanskrit word *advaita,* meaning – in essence – 'not two'. It's an indication of the whole-ness of everything we encounter. For example: no separation between spiritual and secular; no division between outward success and failure. Just an integrated, fully whole sense of being in the world, fully alive, fully present.

EXERCISE 3

Meditation foundations

For this exercise, we'll be breaking down our meditation practice into steps. As always, you don't have to stick rigidly to this set of steps. Try it out, see how you feel – and if you want to change it up, do it. It's important that these practices (or any other wellness practice while we're at it) serve *you*, not the other way around. Life's too short, and there are far too many alternative options, to keep plodding along with an exercise or practice that isn't really bringing you any benefits. With that said, here are the steps.

Step 1: Space

Decide where you're going to be for your meditation. There are no strict rules – many traditions advocate for a seated, still prac-tice, but you can incorporate meditation into other activities, or into gentle movement like walking or stretching (the central theme of yoga, at least in its Western form, is to incorporate a meditative element into a sequence of movement).

So, decide where you'll be – and notice your environment. If you're at home, make an effort to distinguish your meditation space from your daily lifestyle. It's much easier to dive into meditation if you have a welcoming, supportive space around you – think comfortable seating, or a clean, organized environment – although, of course, it is possible to meditate within the chaos of everyday life. If you're not at home (for example, if you're on a train or walking), observe the environment around you before you begin. What can you notice? How can you make your space as comfortable and supportive as possible? Sometimes the smallest actions – even just adjusting your position or putting on a warm jumper – can make the biggest differences.

Step 2: Silence

Again, we're going to be interpreting this in a flexible way. Instead of pure silence, you can simply observe the sounds around you, and then allow them to form the framework for your meditation. In this way, even though you may not sit in perfect 'silence', you're still creating a mindful space – one in which you're aware of your environment. If we're trying to settle our minds, we can easily get annoyed by external sounds, as if they're intentionally designed to disrupt our serenity. In fact, it's the opposite – we can actually welcome these sounds *into* the structure of our meditation itself.

A quick example, if this is all sounding a little unrealistic. Let's say you sit down to meditate and you hear a conversation in the next room. Our instinct is probably to focus on the noise – to figure out what they're talking about, and then (if we're honest) to wish that they'd stop. But, even though this *feels like* you're helping your meditation by wishing for silence, the resistance against the present moment – with all of its sounds and irritations and discomforts – is taking you farther away from the practice.

So, what should you do? Instead of resisting your circumstances, or wishing they were different, or even moving your location to find a more 'perfect' place for your practice, see if you can just let things rest as they are. This is sometimes known as leaning into 'what is' – a simple idea, but hard to implement. In the example above, it involves making the sounds a part of your meditation practice, allowing yourself to be fully present and aware of them, and treating them as the foundation on which to build your practice. Allow the noise to wash over you without fighting it. Try to let go of any tension that has built up in your physical body – your shoulders, jawline or upper back. In meditation, it's sometimes said that the art of the practice is embracing the present moment *as if you had chosen it for yourself.* That's a radical thought, in many ways. It's a level of acceptance that not only includes allowing things to be the way that they are, but actively incorporating them into the way you would design your own life, given freedom of choice. We'll come back to that idea a little later, but for now, let's go to Step 3.

Step 3: Stillness

Just like Step 2, we're not talking about 'stillness' in its literal sense. 'Stillness', for the purposes of this meditation practice, focuses more on mental stillness: stillness of the mind or stillness of your thoughts.

Try this: pause for a moment, and sit with your own thoughts. Give yourself no longer than a minute to try it. And notice, as you sit and think, how many things are moving through your mind, and how fast they're moving. Maybe you're thinking about work, or about other people, or about something you need to do later, or what you're having for dinner. Or, more likely, you're thinking about a mix of all of these things, each one passing through your mind at a million miles an hour. This is the nature of our thoughts – they tend to be fleeting, fast-paced and frantic. It's not a bad thing that we default to this mode of thinking, either. I'm sure you can think of a handful of situations in which this mind-based, racing style of thoughts might be *just* the thing you need in that moment. Reacting to a threatening or dangerous situation, for example. Thinking about how to respond in a flowing conversation. Coming up with new ideas, or new plans, or inventing solutions to problems. Our fast-paced mode of thinking is undeniably useful to us, in countless moments of our everyday lives. But it's not the *only* way we can use our thoughts.

In the best-selling psychology book *Thinking, Fast and Slow*, Daniel Kahneman looks at a similar topic from a behavioural perspective. Kahneman introduces two main 'systems' of thought. System 1 operates 'automatically and quickly, with little or no effort and no sense of voluntary control'.[8] Recall the experience we had above, where you allowed your mind to wander, make judgements, work on intuition – this is one example of System 1 in action (there are many others, of course). System 2, on the other hand, is associated with the 'subjective experience of agency, choice and concentration'. This is more reflective thought: complex problem-solving, effortful thought, considered judgement. System 2 takes energy and intention. System 1, in some cases, is a short cut.

This comparison – the two 'systems', thinking fast and thinking slow – isn't exactly how traditional meditation teaching characterizes the mind, but it's a helpful template for distinguishing our 'fast, frantic thinking' from our 'meditative, reflective thinking'. In meditation, we're seeking stillness of the mind; a wholly different experience. One of the ways in which this departs from Kahneman's two systems is that our 'meditative mind' is intended to be relaxed, open and gentle. We're not intently focused on achieving or solving anything. Instead, we let the thoughts pass over us, without giving them too much attention or concern.

Let's try one more exercise, to finish up this step and before we tie it all together. Just as before, pause for a moment. But this time, instead of letting your mind race away, *observe* what comes up, as if you were watching it from outside of your own mind. You can use a visualization, if it helps – notice the thoughts coming and going (perhaps like water running in a stream, or like clouds passing on a windy day, if either of those images works for you). Without judgement, just see what arises. And then gently let it pass, without holding on to it or analysing it, or, really, thinking critically about it in any way.

THE THREE STEPS IN ACTION

First, locate your space. Get settled, wherever you are. Notice your surroundings, and then bring your attention to your breath.

Second, observe the sounds around you. Let them fall into the space of your meditation, almost as if you had chosen them voluntarily. If you feel an emotional reaction arising as you hear a sound (annoyance or irritation, for example), notice it and then see if you can let it pass.

Third, settle your thoughts. You can close your eyes, if it feels comfortable, or simply 'soften' your gaze – which means, in essence, looking at something without focusing on it. When thoughts come, as they inevitably will, just notice them. Don't engage with them, don't dive into them, and – perhaps most importantly – don't judge yourself for having them. Just let them settle, and then let them pass when they're ready. If the same thoughts keep arising, use them as part of the practice: each time you notice the thought, it gives you another opportunity to return to a place of stillness.

After you've set up the three foundational steps, give yourself a period of time in which to complete your meditation (say, ten or fifteen minutes). You can set up a timer beforehand, or just gently bring yourself out of meditation when you're ready. It's often nice to transition back into your day with a little physical movement – take a stretch, or roll your shoulders in a slow, circular motion. Give yourself time to 're-enter' your day: move slowly, make a note of anything you observed during your meditation, and set a time to return for your next practice.

At the beginning of your journey into meditative practice, it's a good idea to practise every day – it helps to establish the habit and gives you a more tangible sense of the benefits over time. But, once you're a seasoned meditator, you'll most likely be able to find meditative moments within your everyday life, without necessarily needing to sit down for a seated practice every day. You might, for example, only sit in meditation practice a few times a week but engage with other forms of meditation more regularly – for example, meditative walking, or yoga, or other practices like mindfulness (more on that one later). Or perhaps, you might make it a committed daily practice, in the more traditional sense. It's your life, after all. Only you get to decide what works best.

■ ▬▬▬▬▬▬▬▬▬▬▬▬▬▬ ■

Contemplation and knowledge

As with many of the ideas in this book, the principle of 'wholeness' shows up in various forms, in various traditions. One example, from the Christian mystical tradition ('mystical', here, meaning a method of thought intended to enhance contact with a 'greater being'[9]), is the practice of *contemplation*. In a similar way to meditation, contemplation is designed to bring the practitioner closer to the knowledge of reality. This sounds like an ambitious – and slightly strange – goal: after all, don't we encounter reality every single day, just by simply being here? The theologian and philosopher Augustine of Hippo drew the following distinction between two types of knowledge: a type of knowledge known by reason and rationality (he called this *scientia*), and a type of knowledge known by wisdom (he called this *sapientia*). In other words, you can 'know' reality in two ways: through your mind, by thinking and reasoning and puzzling things out, or through your very being, by having a direct, personal encounter with the world.[10]

There's a widely circulated quote that goes something like this: '*The longest distance in the world is the distance from your mind to your heart.*' Sounds a bit clichéd, but this is the kind of idea we're getting at here: the ability to 'know' something in your head and then translate that into fully embodied, fully felt knowledge. Perhaps we could call this latter type of knowledge 'living knowledge', to be contrasted with 'learned knowledge'. But before we get too caught up in the idea of mystical thinking, wholeness and 'living knowledge', let's jump into a practical example of contemplation practice.

▌ EXERCISE 4 ▌

Contemplation basics

Before we get started, and to give you some essential context, let's take a quick look at the history and development of this practice. Contemplative prayer arose out of earlier 'mystical' traditions, which were, in themselves, a rebellion against the rules and regulations of society. Monasticism, in the Western tradition, emerged around the third century ce, with early members of monastic communities escaping everyday life to live alone in the desert. (The word 'monk' actually derives from the Greek word *monakhos*, 'solitary', itself derived from *monos*, 'alone'.) The original idea of the monastic lifestyle was to get closer to God by abandoning pretty much everything else – social ties, relationships with others, comfortable living. The earliest monks, grouped around Egypt and Syria, escaped to the desert, living in caves and wandering the land, often gathering together for prayer services. This stripped-back, minimal way of living has formed the inspiration for a huge number of communities and theologians.

One of these theologians was a man named Benedict of Nursia, who shaped some of the early ideas of monasticism into a more settled community. This 'Benedictine monasticism' is probably more what you imagine when you think of the monastic lifestyle (robes, monasteries and so on), and

Benedictine communities still exist across the world today. And – we're circling back to it now – one of the core practices of these 'settled' monastic communities was *contemplation*.

Contemplation is practised in many ways, in many different forms, and is incorporated into a monk's timetable at regular intervals. When I trained among a 'new monastic' community (which drew on Benedictine practices, among others), we usually practised contemplative meditation several times a day: in the morning, before breakfast; at midday, before lunch; and in the evening, before bed. This kind of structure is helpful because these are parts of the day that lend themselves well to natural pauses, and they're *also* times of the day when you might have a routine you can slot your contemplative practice into. It's easy to lose track of time during an afternoon, for example, but you normally tap back into some kind of wind-down routine in the evening – and that's where your practice can be brought in.

A basic contemplative practice involves the following elements:

- silence or stillness
- prayerful reading or reflection on a sacred text
- observation or awareness
- peaceful resting in the present moment.

To practise a non-religious form of contemplation, you might take the following steps:

1. Find a comfortable place to sit, somewhere you're unlikely to be disturbed. Search out as much stillness as you can.
2. Next, find a piece of text, a phrase or a short poem to focus your attention. Look for something of meaning or personal

significance. Read it a few times. Turn the words over in your mind.

3. Placing the words aside, allow your mind to come fully into the present moment. Don't try to do anything (don't even try to clear your mind). Just pause and allow yourself to settle.

4. If you'd like to practise an attitude of surrender, you can visualize a 'letting go' sensation – letting go of thoughts, of effort, of restriction, of goals and ambitions. You don't necessarily have to be offering yourself up in a religious sense, here – you can simply cultivate a position of open submission to the present moment.

5. After a few minutes (around ten minutes should work well), you can slowly bring your awareness back into your body, stretch, open your eyes, and begin to transition back into your day.

At this point, you might be wondering what the difference is, then, between meditation and contemplation. Aside from the obvious difference in tradition, cultural background and religious heritage, there are some other distinctions. First, meditation often utilizes some form of human effort, whereas contemplation is more of a 'letting go' or a 'surrendering' to the practice. (This is, of course, a generalization – there is a huge variety of practices, both within meditation and within contemplation – but it can be helpful to make the distinction in broad terms.)

Second, contemplation often leads to action (i.e. a changed behaviour or new attitude to life), whereas meditation may be practised as a goal in itself (i.e. the practice itself is the focus, rather than any inspiration or revelation that arises as a result).

Third, contemplation is often thought of as a 'turning outward' – a making of space for personal transformation, while meditation is often thought of as a 'turning inward' (again, using a generalized example of a typical practice).

As with most types of spiritual or reflective practice, there are valuable things to be found on all sides. The question, as ever, is which practice works best for you, and your task is to experiment, to try new things, until you find it.

Before we go on

As we discussed at the start of this chapter, this work – the work of meaning, purpose, mental wellbeing and existential fulfilment – is challenging. Not just because it takes time and effort (which it does), but *also* because the results aren't immediately evident in our daily lives. It's much harder to see the outcome of, for example, a consistent meditation or purpose-focused practice than it is to see the results of a consistent fitness workout, or a creative project that you dedicate your time towards. But the transformation, even if only gradually perceptible, is there.

This type of work is intended to be foundation-building: it can give you the structure and fundamental architecture upon which to build your life. While it may not be directly linked to recovery from specific mental health conditions, it can form a more continuous part of a daily wellbeing practice. And although it might not feel like you're doing much at all, as you go deeper into these practices, and reach farther into your own existential experience, the distance you've already travelled will become clearer.

CHAPTER 5

Body

● ● ●

The global 'wellness' economy is valued at around $4 trillion.[1] Just in case you find that impossibly large number hard to imagine, a trillion has 12 zeros. *Twelve.* This is an industry, then, that profits from our eternal search for 'being well'. For this industry to flourish, it's not enough that we know the basics. We're all aware we need to get more sleep and eat some vegetables. The global wellness industry isn't really about that. It's about finding the secret, the fast-track, the short-cut solution to an ever-increasing standard of elite wellbeing.

So, in this chapter, we'll explore what it really means to 'be well'. Deeper than aesthetics, or image, or specific diets, or expensive wellness trends, this work is about embodiment, being present, the mind–body connection, and what it really means to practise 'care for the self'. Drawing on my background in fitness, yoga and other disciplines, we'll be moving through a variety of practices, many of them with surprising similarities and consistent themes.

Before we begin

First, a quick note on how the practices in this chapter differ from similar trends you might find within the wellness industry. As with most lifestyle habits and choices, the practices themselves might look similar. It's the *intention* behind the practices that determines how they take effect in your life. In other words, you can do meditation with the intention of being calmer as you file your work emails, or to help you clear your mind before a meeting with your boss. *Or*, you can use the exact same practice – in this example, meditation – to dive deeper into your own experience of existing in the world, or your connection to your body, or your sense of self and purpose.

At least in the context of this book, there's no 'right' or 'wrong' way to use this work. Once you've explored a discipline, you're free to choose how to integrate it into your life. Bear in mind, though, that many of these practices have deep, meaningful traditions and histories behind them – elements that the modern wellbeing industry often overlooks – and it's always worth going one layer deeper. This chapter (and the Resources section at the end of the book) are intended to form only a starting point.

Welcome home

I wonder if you remember the first time you thought about your body, from an external perspective. Because, of course, we all started off living *within* our bodies, inextricably connected to the experience of being alive. As children, we needed sleep, food and movement and responded to our own physical cues in an instinctive way. But, at some point, we became conscious of ourselves: of our bodies, as distinct from our minds and our thoughts and our intentions. Over time, we gain a growing awareness of how we look compared to others. We see ourselves in mirrors and photographs, and we make decisions or criticisms or judgements about what we find. By the time we become adults, we often accept this separation without question, seeing our bodies as tools to be improved or enhanced, but less often seeing them as a home. And there's no one we can blame for this, specifically. For sure, our social values have a part in the disconnect. (It certainly pays corporations well if we all remain slightly dissatisfied with whatever we have – always wanting something else, something that remains just out of reach.) But it's hard to assign blame exclusively to current social structures. Perhaps we could blame our parents, or the media, or celebrities, or technology, or ourselves. But none of this offers us what we actually need, which is – in the end – a path back to ourselves.

In this chapter, we'll dive into some of the practices surrounding embodiment, and we'll see what we can learn from some more traditional practices – yoga, mindful movement, body scans and so on. But these practices are intended more as a *reminder* than as a wholly new teaching. We already know what it feels like to be in our bodies, to move and sense and experience the world. For most of us, it's difficult *not* to experience some element of embodiment every day. Our shoulders ache, or our feet hurt, or we get hungry or thirsty or tired. Our bodies are constantly reminding us of their presence. The difference is, for most of us, that we respond from a position of *separation* instead of *integration*. Our instinctive approach is to see the body as something that belongs to us – a separate entity that we can perfect and sculpt and shape and look at from a distance. But we're *here*, in our bodies, in this experience of our own lives, every waking moment. And so, these practices are just a reminder – to come back to ourselves, whenever we forget.

There's a quote, often circulated in yoga classes, that sums up this idea. The quote goes something like this:

'The body is a constant reminder of present moment awareness, because the body can only be in the present moment. The mind switches between past and future. But the body is only ever present.'[2]

We'll explore this a little more as we move through this chapter, but for now – just to sum up this idea – the body can become your anchor to the present moment. And it's still there to remind you, every single time you forget.

Embodiment

Embodiment, in this context, doesn't have a set definition. We could describe it as the 'personal relationship' to our body, or – more simply – the way we sense our own body, and the way we feel about it. Perhaps, then, we could separate out two elements here: first, the sensory connection to our own bodies, and second, the way we feel or perceive that connection. It sounds straightforward (surely, we feel what's happening within our own bodies, right?), but our everyday pace of life often separates us from ourselves, on an embodied, physical level. I'm sure you've had days like this: rushing from one thing to another, skipping breaks to save time, ignoring signs of anxiety or stress or exhaustion because there's simply too much to get done. In *The Body Keeps the Score*,[3] the psychiatrist Bessel van der Kolk writes (in the context of trauma therapy) that 'when our senses become muffled, we no longer feel fully alive'. This is evident in the process of trauma recovery, but it's true, to some extent, for all of us. When we get separated from the real, feeling, sensing entity of our human body, we get separated from the depths of our own lives.

With all that in mind, let's explore a few practices that we can use to deepen, strengthen and support our connection to ourselves, our minds and – most importantly – our bodies. This type of work isn't necessarily a strict regime we need to undertake every day. Instead, think of these practices as your foundations, the fundamental building blocks of an enduring sense of embodiment. These are practices to learn, explore and incorporate into your portfolio, and draw upon in the months and years to come. It's less about overnight transformation and more about steadily going deeper into the experience of being within your physical self – a journey that is, at times, challenging, but ultimately one of the most interesting, fulfilling paths to pursue.

Moving

The idea of a 'moving meditation' is often associated with yoga, and with the unity of breath and body (the Sanskrit word *yoga* has its roots in terms meaning 'union' or 'join', in the sense of bringing elements together). But mindful movement, in a broader sense, shows up in a lot of different disciplines. In fact, using a general definition of 'mindfulness' – for example, the definition provided by Jon Kabat-Zinn (the founder of mindfulness-based stress reduction and formerly a leading Western mindfulness practitioner) – it's fully possible to practise mindful movement doing *any* type of physical activity. Let's break down the components of mindfulness, and then we'll work through a few ways to bring mindfulness to your movement, whether you're running a marathon or simply running yourself a bath.

MINDFULNESS

By now, most of us are familiar with the idea of mindfulness: the practice of awareness, through paying attention to the present moment, without judgement.

Let's begin by breaking down the concept. The five main components of mindfulness (in our current context) are:

1. awareness
2. through attention
3. on purpose
4. in the present moment
5. without judgement.

Taken together, we could say that 'mindfulness' is the practice of awareness, through intentionally paying attention to the present moment, and doing so without judgement. As Jon Kabat-Zinn writes in the foundational text *Full Catastrophe Living*, mindfulness is 'moment-to-moment non-judgmental awareness'.[4]

That final element – the non-judgement requirement – is often overlooked, even by regular meditators. As we explored in Chapter 4, our modern minds are pre-programmed for immediate, quick, effective judgements. We *need* this skill to go about our daily lives. But, in the context of mindfulness, it's part of the condition of the practice itself that we exercise non-judgement – towards ourselves and others, and towards the practice itself. This means, for example, that instead of *reacting* to all of the thoughts that arise when you practise meditation (whether you responded to that email or not, for example, or what you're making for breakfast), you simply *observe* these thoughts, without any criticism or analysis. And this, more than any other element of mindfulness, can be the most challenging aspect. It's exhausting to maintain an attitude as countercultural as non-judgement, and it can feel boring to try and try again to cultivate it. But, for the purposes of developing a mindfulness practice, and as Kabat-Zinn reports telling his own patients, *'you don't have to like it; you just have to do it'* (!).[5]

Let's bring it back to the body. The next few exercises will cover some basic mindful movement practices, and your challenge is to integrate these into your regular daily routine for the next few weeks. Once you've mastered the basic practice (in other words, the techniques needed to practise mindful movement), you can depart from these basic practices and instead bring an element of mindful movement to whatever physical activities you enjoy.

EXERCISE 1

The spine stretch

Example of standing alignment   Example of flexion and extension

Your spine is the central supporting structure of your body and, unsurprisingly, plays a huge role in almost every movement you make. It's made up of 33 bones (your vertebrae), which, for the purposes of this exercise, you can think about in three main sections: your upper back, your mid-back and your lower back. These main sections work together, in unity, to allow you to move, bend, swivel, jump, stretch, and do pretty much anything else you want to do with your whole body.

For the purposes of this mindful spinal stretch, we'll be focusing on one main movement: *flexion and extension* (otherwise known as a forward-bend and a back-bend). We'll work through the basics of the movement practice first, and then we'll bring in the element of mindfulness.

The movement

Stand up straight, with your spine in a neutral position. We all have a natural curve to our backs, but as we stand up straight, we're looking for optimal alignment. ('Optimal alignment' is a term that tends to show up in practices such as Pilates and means, essentially, that the body is positioned in such a way that the joints are supported, and any excessive use of force on muscles or joints is reduced.[6]) For most of us, we can get there by standing 'tall' (a feeling of 'lifting' through the spine, while relaxing the shoulders) and positioning our body weight equally through the feet, taking them hip-width apart. Your pelvis is placed in 'neutral', which means that your lower back is neither arched out nor tucked in (instead, it's usually somewhere in the middle).

In modern yoga practice, this kind of pose is known as *Tadasana* (from the Sanskrit term), or 'mountain pose': standing tall, with your arms by your sides and your weight well distributed through the soles of your feet. You should feel as though your spine is anchored through the central line of your body, and your feet should feel stable, grounded and secure. Take a few moments to focus on your breath, which is traditionally – for yoga and meditation practices – brought in and out through your nose.

From here, bend your knees and fold forwards. Start by tucking your chin to your chest, and then see if you can roll down your spine, one bone at a time, until you're folding forwards over bent knees. You can rest your ribs and chest on your thighs, while you allow your spine to curve over. This is known as *flexion* of the spine. When you're ready, after a few deep breaths, start to roll back up. Begin with your lower back – the first few vertebrae stacking on top of each other first – and then your mid-back, followed by your upper back and neck. The head comes up last and you return to your neutral standing position.

Next, take your hands to your hips. From here, see if you can lift up a little through your spine and then bend slightly backwards, as if you're opening the centre of your chest to the ceiling. Don't go anywhere that feels painful or constricted in the lower back – even a few inches of a back-bend is enough. This is known as *extension* of the spine. Take a few breaths in this position and then return to neutral.

The mindfulness

Starting from your standing position, we're going to take those two movements again – but this time, we'll be bringing in those five elements of mindfulness (which are, as a reminder, awareness, attention, purpose, presence and non-judgement).

Begin to roll down the spine, noticing how it feels in your body. If your mind immediately starts to wander (or if you feel bored or uncomfortable), return to the physical sensations in the body, trying to concentrate your mind on those alone.

If it helps to keep you focused, you can ask yourself: *How does this movement feel in my body, right now?* You might have a specific answer to that question (for example, it might feel heavy or light, cold or warm, tight or expansive), or not. Maybe it doesn't really feel like anything, or you can't find the right words to describe it. That's OK as well. Both of these outcomes – both sensation and absence of sensation – are part of the practice of mindful awareness.

When you reach the forward folding position, let your spine relax into the position of *flexion* and bring your awareness to what it feels like in your body, at that moment. Again, you might use a word or phrase to describe it, but you don't have to; if it's easier just to rest in the feeling or sensation at that moment, allow yourself time to do that. Notice, too, the uncomfortable feelings: if there's a tightness or restriction in the spine, or if it feels like a lot of effort to hold the forward fold for a few breaths, notice that.

Mindfulness (and meditation in general) isn't designed to be a universally joyful, enlightening experience, despite the ads you might see for the latest meditation app. Mindfulness can be difficult, exhausting, boring, uncomfortable and seemingly pointless. It's the commitment to the practice – and, importantly, the non-judgement element – that opens the door to the true benefits of the discipline (namely, a more present, embodied experience of being alive, with all the complexities and frustrations that can bring).

As you roll back up towards standing, notice the vertebrae of your back stacking on top of each other, one at a time. Here, you can visualize 'rebuilding' or 'reconstructing' the body, almost as if you were standing up for the first time and you wanted to arrive to stand with lightness and precision.

You can also visualize, as you stand, placing an inch of space between every bone of your spine, so that you finish the rolling up movement with a little more length and expansion. Then, begin the slight bend backwards into 'extension', lengthening your spine into a small back-bend. As you do this, bring your awareness to the space across the front of your chest: as you bend back, you should also feel expansion through the front of your body. You might also bring your awareness to your shoulders, as they roll back, or the front of your throat and neck, as you gently tilt your head back and up. And then, after a few intentional breaths, return to standing in your starting position.

What we've been doing, here, is taking a very basic stretch ('flexion' and 'extension', sometimes also called the 'roll down' in classical Pilates) and adding a layer of awareness – or 'mindful movement'. The simplicity of the stretch is a huge benefit when you're starting out with mindful movement, because the body can find its own rhythm without too much effort or exertion, and you can focus on layering in the mindful awareness.

It's a good idea to incorporate something like this into your routine with regularity: try starting every day with a gentle roll down and roll up, working the spine through flexion and extension. Or you can close your day with this kind of practice, bringing your awareness to how the body feels before you go to sleep. Either way, find a routine you can maintain, and integrate this practice into your life over the course of a few weeks. Some studies indicate it takes around 66 days to form a consistent habit, so *at least* this long to start with.[7]

Once you have the basics of mindful movement in your practice, and you feel comfortable with a simple stretch (as in the example above), see if you can apply the principles to another form of movement practice. Whatever you enjoy doing – running, swimming, walking, or even more basic everyday tasks like cooking or cleaning – see if you can layer in those elements of mindfulness. Awareness, attention, purpose, presence and non-judgement: these are your foundations, and you can apply them wherever you like.

For example, let's say you make your bed every morning. For many of us, this is an instinctive task, in which the body defaults to memory and routine. But to bring an element of mindful awareness to the moment might just provide a deeper experience. Instead of simply making your bed, stretching to adjust pillows, or shaking out your duvet, you can ask yourself: *What does it feel like to move, in this moment?* You can scan through the body, noticing how the movements feel – is it effortful or light? Is the body tired or energized? Is there any discomfort, or does it feel easy? And then, of course, that final element of non-judgement. Whatever you discover about your body during the exercise, you accept it as part of the experience of the practice, and of being alive. There are no 'bad' outcomes. There's simply a whole spectrum of sensation and feeling, all of which is part of the process of being a living, sensing, feeling human. And – linking to the other ideas in this book – this is the depth and quality of life that we're looking for. Not just a simple surface-level experience (the kind of glowing, filtered bodies you might see on social media), but a genuine, authentic, personal experience of being *right here*, in our own lives, in our own physical bodies.

One last note about the mindful movement practice before we move on. The idea of moving 'mindfully' can sometimes seem a bit naive, or overly simple, when it comes to the complexities and difficulties of being a human being. Often, we don't actually *want* to be mindful about our own bodies, or we don't want to be fully aware of the sensations of movement. You only have to look at the traditional coping mechanisms of the modern world to see that they're mostly aligned towards 'checking out' – whether it's through an unwinding drink at the end of the day, or online shopping, or scrolling social media. Sometimes even things we think of as 'wellness' can have that numbing element to them: it's wholly possible to tap out of our real, lived experience as humans in favour of buying the latest wellbeing product, or forcing ourselves through a set exercise regime that doesn't have any relationship to our actual physical feelings.

In other words: it's tricky to stay put, to stay present. As much as we can appreciate our aliveness, we often don't want to fully be *in* it. And it seems too simple to say this is all solved by becoming 'aware' of our present experience. But, importantly, mindfulness is not just about a few moments of awareness. As Jon Kabat-Zinn writes, *'the work of growth and healing takes time. It requires patience and consistency in the meditation practice over a period of weeks, if not months and years'.* And while Jon Kabat-Zinn's writing relates to pain reduction, it applies to any form of mindful awareness practice that we encounter. It's not a simple, quick-fix solution to feeling 'better'. (You might not even immediately feel better – and, even if you do, it's not a sign that you've 'completed' the task.) What you're trying to encounter is a real, fully embodied experience of being *right here*, in the body you're in right now, and being open to whatever it is that comes up for you when you feel it.

In yoga, teachers often say that you bring your 'whole self' with you to the mat when you come to practise. I think this is easily interpreted on a superficial level: sure, we bring ourselves to the yoga practice with aches and pains, with injuries or experience, with energy or exhaustion. That's true. But we also bring our 'whole selves' with us to the mat in terms of our embodied experience. We bring all the parts of ourselves that *don't* want to be acknowledged. We bring the discomfort with being in our own skin. We bring all the elements of ourselves that we wish weren't there, or that we'd rather overlook. At the heart of it, this is an idea about full presence in the world: being *right here*, and taking up the space to allow yourself to do it. And the intention, with your mindful movement practice, is to take that idea of presence – in your body and beyond – back into the world with you. It's not only designed for that three-minute spine stretch in the morning. It's designed to spill over, eventually, into the rest of your life.

EXERCISE 2

Body scans

Let's stay with the theme of mindfulness for a final exercise and work through a body scan practice. You might be familiar with this practice, perhaps from yoga or meditation, but we'll look at it in the context of cultivating *aliveness*. The body scan is a great exercise to include in your portfolio, largely due to its ability to reconnect you with every aspect of your physical self. Most often, we think about the parts of the body that bother us: maybe you have an injury that causes pain, or an ache in your shoulders after a day at your desk. Maybe there are parts of your body you wish you could change, or parts of your body that you prefer not to think about, as if they could be removed from your existence altogether. On the other hand, there might be parts of your body that you love; parts that you take any opportunity to display or enjoy. None of this is bad (or good). Coming back to that idea of non-judgemental awareness, we're exploring how to integrate *all* of it. The parts of the body that feel uncomfortable, and the parts you're proud of. All of it belongs. And the body scan is a great (and short!) practice to begin to bring it all back together.

The body scan is best performed when you're still: either lying down or seated tends to work well. If you're sitting in a chair, place the soles of your feet on the floor and your hands on your lap or gently by your sides. If you're sitting on the floor, you could try leaning against a wall for support. And if you're lying down, make sure you're comfortable, with your arms and legs supported. Give yourself a 15-minute window to try the full practice and – ideally – try to be somewhere you won't be easily disturbed.

The practice is fairly simple: you intentionally and carefully bring your whole awareness to each part of the body, beginning with the soles of your feet and working all the way up to the crown of your head. You go slowly, 'scanning' each part of the body in turn. And the real skill is to *pay attention*. Just as we did in the mindful movement practice, you're noticing what it feels like in each part of the body, one part at a time, until you've covered every inch of yourself. And, just as in the mindful movement practice, you're doing the whole thing with no judgement. Whatever sensation you find, you invite it into the practice, as part of the integrated, holistic experience of being alive.

So, start with the soles of your feet. Scan up and down the soles of your feet to see what you can feel. If your feet are against the floor, notice the sensation of the ground underneath your feet. What does it feel like? What's the specific experience of the soles of your feet, in this precise moment? If you're wearing shoes or socks, what does that feel like? Can you name it? Could you describe it? As with all mindfulness practices, it doesn't matter if you don't know exactly what it feels like, or even if it feels like nothing at all. This is all part of the practice – it all belongs.

Take the same approach as you scan up your legs, into your knees, and then farther up into your hips and lower abdomen. You might, at some point, encounter a part of the body that feels uncomfortable to acknowledge, or a part that you don't want to focus on. For the purposes of this practice, just observe that sensation. You don't have to force yourself to do anything, or to notice or feel anything in particular. If you meet resistance during the practice, that resistance *is* the practice – or, at least, it becomes part of the practice. Again, all of it belongs. You simply observe the feeling of resistance and then you move onwards.

As you scan farther up the body, into your chest and lungs, you can focus on your breath – the simplicity of the inhale and the exhale. You can notice the rise and fall of your chest, or any sensations that accompany the breath in your body (for example, openness or restriction, steadiness or speed). After observing the breath for a few moments, take your body scan down into your arms – you can do one at a time or both at once – and then farther into your hands, palms and fingertips. If your hands are resting on your body, observe the feeling. If your palms are turned upwards, see if you can scan them for sensation. Again, if you don't feel anything, the absence of sensation is the thing to notice.

Once you finish scanning your hands, travel back up your arms and into your shoulders, then to the back of the neck, and then to the top of your head. From here, take a full scan of the entire body, encompassing every single piece of yourself. You can use the breath to do it: scan down as you breathe out and scan back up as you breathe in. Take a good few minutes to finish your body scan, staying in silence and stillness for a while if you can, before bringing some movement back to the body and continuing your day.

You might, at this point, feel any number of emotions. It's possible you'll be bored, or restless, or ready to get up and get moving. It's possible that you fell asleep during the process. It's possible that you feel a sense of wholeness and integration, like your entire body is alive and energized and belongs fully to you. All of this is possible. As usual, with meditation or mindfulness practice, the outcome is less relevant than the practice itself. If you take regular body scans, you'll have some days that feel fantastic and some days that feel lethargic. Some days, you might end up feeling worse than when you started. Other days, you'll feel like your practice placed you on top of the world.

This depth of mindfulness practice – the idea that the practice has value *beyond* the outcome – isn't often spoken about. We don't usually want to spend time on practices that don't carry a predictably good outcome (in other words, things that don't reliably make us feel 'better'). But this, in the end, is the real experience of being alive: not always maintaining a constant state of physical perfection, but just being *here*, fully alive, and letting that be enough (or, really, more than enough).

Breathing

Pause, for a moment, and observe your own breath. See if you can watch the breath as it moves through your body, without controlling or changing it, or trying to alter its natural rhythm. If your mind wanders, bring it back to the simple act of breathing in and out. This basic, instinctive function – the very symbol of the life running through us – is so easily forgotten, other than in times of physical stress (for example, a high-adrenaline situation, or a form of intense exercise, or even during a physiological response like a panic attack). But the breath is one of the central reminders of our existence, grounded in the body, anchoring us to the present moment and to our embodied reality. So it's worth paying attention: on a basic level, to cultivate appreciation for our own exist-ence, and on a deeper level, to develop the skill of paying attention (ultimately, so that the breath can become a tool in our portfolio as we continue to pursue a sense of 'aliveness').

In some Indian scriptures, the sacred Hindu texts from which most modern yoga practices draw their roots, the breath is known as *prana*. The word itself, translated from the original Sanskrit, is often said to mean 'life force' or 'vital principle'. The idea of *prana* itself is much more than physiological breath (in other words, the mechanical process of breathing in and out). In various ways, *prana* is used to symbolize the energy of consciousness, or the creative power of the self, or – on a more cosmic level – the energy of the universe itself. For the yoga tradition, *prana* forms one of the eight 'limbs' of the practice (alongside other elements like abstinence and meditation). In the context of the eight limbs, as formulated by the ancient Indian sage Patanjali, *prana* shows up in breathing exercises, also known as *pranayama* (from *prana*, meaning 'breath', and *ayama*, meaning 'restraint', although translations vary). The yoga tradition offers a whole host of practices for mastering control of the breath, and this work is seen as an essential step on the path to achieving inner and outer harmony.[8]

A similar idea shows up in other religious and philosophical contexts. The Greek word *pneuma* carries a comparable range of translations (breath; life force; human spirit) and shows up across Stoic philosophy, Christianity and Judaism. All of these uses share the idea of *pneuma* representing an active, driving, creative force, expressed in the human body through the inhale and the exhale. And the same ideas – of life-giving power or physical vitality – show up here as well. In addition, there's a general acknowledgement that the breath is something sacred; that it represents something above and beyond ourselves; that it's not just a biological function to be ignored, but something to be valued and noticed and celebrated.

With all that in mind, here's a quick breathing exercise.

EXERCISE 3

The box breath

For this exercise, make sure you're sitting or lying down comfortably and that you're unlikely to be disturbed. You don't need a long time to practise breathwork, in general, but it helps to have at least five minutes to settle in. You can also do a simple breath practice before you sleep, which is – aside from being a time when you're unlikely to be disturbed – a great way to ease into falling asleep.

Begin by closing your eyes, or unfocusing your gaze. Then, imagine you have the shape of a box on your chest. The box has four long, equal sides: one across the top of your chest (parallel to your shoulders), one down the right-hand side of your chest (parallel with the side of your waist), one across the bottom (parallel with your hips) and one up the left-hand side of your chest (parallel with the other side of your waist). For this exercise, you're going to visualize breathing around the sides of the box.

Start by taking a deep breath out, to empty the lungs. Then, breathe in. Imagine the inhale is travelling up one side of the box (you can choose which one). Once you reach the top, hold your breath. Imagine travelling across the top line of the box. As you exhale, imagine travelling your breath down the other side of the box. And as you reach the end of your exhale, hold your breath and imagine it travelling across the bottom of your box. Then, continue for a few rounds. You can choose whether to keep a consistent pace or whether to slow down, gradually, so the sides of the box become longer and longer. Continue for the duration of your practice (five or ten minutes is usually a good length) and then return your attention to simply breathing in and out, before finishing.

This technique (which, by the way, is reported to be used by US Navy SEALs as a method of stress reduction[9]) does a couple of things for you. On a practical level, holding your breath – both at the bottom and the top of the box – increases the amount of carbon dioxide in your lungs, which triggers the cardioinhibitory response (in other words, it has the effect of lowering your heart rate). This, in turn, can help to activate the body's parasympathetic nervous system – your 'rest and digest' phase of being, as opposed to the 'fight or flight' response.[10] On a more *embodied* level, the box breath exercise is a reminder that you have the power to design and shape the creative life force running through your body. It also serves as a reminder of the immense power of the breath, something that we all have in common, and something that orientates us within a long tradition of other people who have moved and breathed and experienced being alive on this planet. (Or you can simply use the breathing exercise to relax. As always, it's up to you.)

A quick story about the breath, before we move on. In the Jewish tradition, the divine name is said to be unutterable – and, when written out, takes the form of a collection of vowels (making it difficult to pronounce, even if you tried). It's said, in some traditions, that this collection of vowels actually symbolizes the sound of the breath. In other words, the sound of your own breathing is the word of God: both the inhale and the exhale make up the name of God, when joined together.[11] And this idea – regardless of whether you're religious or an atheist, or even if you don't really care about symbolic stories at all – is in line with everything else we've explored in this section.

The breath, as simple and obvious as it can feel, is symbolic of something else, something greater. For you, it might be a symbol of the fullness of life, or the creative energy that continues to flow through your body, even at this very moment. Or, following religious or cultural symbolism, you might like the idea of your breath being linked to something sacred: a reminder that you belong to the world in a far greater way than just living a tiny, transient life on a meaningless planet. Or perhaps you use the breath as a tool for simple embodiment, for just being here, in your own physical form, breathing because you *can*, and enjoying your own existence.

Wherever you end up, the breath is worth paying attention to.

The ground of being

We're finishing up this chapter with an exploration of an idea from Existential Analysis (a field of existential therapy, developed by Alfried Längle, drawing on the work of Viktor Frankl but expanding beyond it). This is an idea that addresses the experience of feeling 'grounded' in the world. The overall idea is called the 'ground of being'. (The phrase 'ground of being' often shows up in a spiritual context – for example, the theologian and philosopher Paul Tillich used this phrase as a metaphor for God – but we're looking at it from a slightly different angle.) In Existential Analysis, this concept touches on your ultimate belonging in this world: the sense that you have of belonging here, and that your belonging here can be experienced as a fundamentally *good* thing.

In Existential Analysis, the idea of trusting in the 'ground of being' is described as 'fundamental trust'. Fundamental trust includes a level which contains a 'faithfulness to the self' – having a sense of reliance on yourself, and a deep, inner knowledge that you will stand by yourself unconditionally. And when it comes to the 'ground of being', the concept of fundamental trust reflects an essential and personal sense of self-assurance: the sense that, no matter the challenges or personal circumstances that arise from time to time, there is always solid ground beneath your feet, to give your life support and security.

These ideas might sound a little unfamiliar, because they're not often reflected in the current cultural narrative. They're not religious ideas, although they can certainly exist alongside a theological set of beliefs. And they're not necessarily social concepts, although they might be represented in various traditions and cultural backgrounds. The ideas themselves have more of a transcendent nature: they apply regardless of the circumstances or context. They allow us to find our place in the world despite all the things that have happened to us – good, bad and everything in between – and all the things that are yet to happen to us. And these ideas are not the same as gratitude or self-love. It's deeper than just having a good sense of self-confidence, or liking ourselves, or extending ourselves compassion. This is an enduring, grounded, foundational belief about the world: that it's *OK* to be here, that we fundamentally belong here, and that nothing – no outward intervention, no changes in our luck or fortune, no heartbreak or grief or tragedy – can take that away from us.

I wanted to include these ideas – of fundamental trust and the 'ground of being' – in this body-focused chapter, because it relates closely to our sense of wellbeing in the world. And by 'wellbeing', again, we're not thinking of surface-level aesthetics, fitness goals, or even things like nutrition or health. We're talking more about *how you feel, existentially,* as an individual human being in the world. Because sometimes – and I'd include my own experiences in this – we can feel out of place in the world, like we're not supposed to be here, or that our being here is not fundamentally a good thing. The 'fundamental trust' idea is a movement in the opposite direction: it takes us into full dialogue with the world, so that we take up our space and feel as though we're entitled to do so. It has less to do with what we look like, and how we appear, and more about how we actually perceive our individual place on this planet. And so, it's the foundational element onto which we can build all the other elements of wellbeing. After all, there's not much point in eating a perfect diet, working out every day and living to an impossibly large age if you don't actually feel settled within the world we all call home.

EXERCISE 4

Finding fundamental trust[12]

In Existential Analysis, three conditions are regarded as delivering a sense of fundamental trust: *protection, space* and *support.*[13] Perhaps most obviously, childhood experiences, early family ties and our personal relationships can help to establish (or not) our sense of fundamental trust. Religious beliefs can do this as well: most religions advocate for a sense of 'belonging' in the world (although it's possible, of course, to believe a set of religious principles without actually *experiencing* them as a reality in your own life). But, aside from all of that, fundamental trust can be practised, cultivated and developed over time. Here's a simple exercise to get you started.

For this exercise, sit in a chair with the soles of your feet on the floor. Place your hands on your lap with the palms facing down and close your eyes (or simply 'unfocus' your gaze, if that feels more comfortable). From here, bring your attention to your feet.

As you sit, observe the sensation of the soles of your feet against the ground. Notice whether they feel heavy or light, or whether there are other sensations. Bring your awareness to the stability under your feet. Even if you feel that you're barely resting your feet on the floor, the reality – in physical terms – is that the ground is pressing back against you, with equal force. There isn't really a way of moving through the world without a supporting system under your feet, pushing right back against you. In some senses, then, the world is supporting you with every step you take.

After paying attention to your feet for a few moments,
bring your attention to the palms of your hands. Again, feel
the sensation of the palms pressing against your legs and
notice whether it feels heavy or light, or warm or cool (or
any other appropriate description). Bring yourself *in* to the
feeling, so that you fully feel the weight of one part of your
body resting against another. This, in a way, is another constant source of foundational support, as you move through
the world: the ability to use your physical body to support
and ground yourself.

Finally, bring your attention back and focus on this
single question: *How do I feel as I move through the world?*
To expand, you can ask yourself: Can I find a sense of
fundamental trust in the way things are, a sense that things
are, simply, going to be *OK*, regardless of what happens?
If I don't have a full, constant sense of 'fundamental trust',
can I find pockets of it, or moments where I feel like I'm
grounded or anchored in the world? What am I doing during those moments? Can I create more of these moments in
my everyday life?

After sitting for a few minutes, start to bring a little
movement back to the body, and slowly bring your awareness
back to the space around you. If anything came to mind as
a response to the final part of the exercise, note it down. It
might be that fundamental trust develops for you from time
to time, in certain places and moments, and you can begin to
notice – and then cultivate – a deeper sense of it over a period
of months or years. Or, if no answers came to mind during
the exercise, make it a priority to check in with yourself in the
coming weeks and months. When you do find yourself in an
enjoyable moment, or a moment when you feel fully *yourself,*

make a mental reminder. It's often during the times we feel most energized and excited by life that we can come closer to this sense of fundamental trust. From there, we can work on bringing that sense into our portfolio of skills, helping us develop a feeling of 'aliveness' and belonging at all times – even when external circumstances are not in our favour.

Before we go on

As you'll be starting to recognize, this type of work often runs counter to modern cultural expectations. For many people, a sense of embodiment, or a deep connection to the sensations of the body, is something to be considered only at the extremes of life: moments of pain, for example, or of pleasure. The practices we've covered in this chapter encourage a different path. This is a path that advocates for an enduring, consistent, sustainable approach to physicality, one that reaches out for the fullness of physical experience and embraces all of it – the difficulties and discomforts as well as the joy. As with most of the practices in this book, this might well be the more challenging path, but its rewards are deep, fulfilling and long-lasting.

CHAPTER 6

Work

• • •

Grab a coffee, we're heading into work. In this chapter, we'll be figuring out how to find inspiration and excitement in your working life. We'll look specifically at the idea of the portfolio career, going right back to the time when it was relatively new to think about 'going portfolio'. The 'portfolio' idea has been around for a while, but we'll be exploring it from a variety of new perspectives, including self-employment, corporate careers, side-projects and other non-traditional ways of working. And, even if the portfolio ideas aren't your thing, we'll also dive into tools and techniques to help you find meaning, purpose and *aliveness* at work (of all the places to find it!).

Before we begin

Eighty thousand hours. This is, approximately, the amount of time you'll spend at work during your lifetime. Eighty thousand hours of reading emails, sitting in meeting rooms, listening to calls, fixing typos, talking to colleagues, charming clients, closing deals, designing projects, fixing things – or whatever else it is you happen to do with your working life. Eighty thousand hours of getting things done and putting things off and watching the clock. If you're lucky, some of these hours will give you a sense of fulfilment, or excitement, or purpose. But maybe not.

I started my career in corporate law, which was – in so many ways – a great fit for me. I love to analyse and debate and argue (skills that I put to good use growing up, much to the irritation of my parents). Maybe you had this feeling too, growing up – finding a specific set of skills you were good at, or that you enjoyed working on, and they led you towards a particular career path. For me, it was law – studying, at first, and then into the corporate world. I soon realized, though, that the real world of work was nowhere near as straightforward as those early years of reading and studying. When we start a job, even one that links directly from our studies or training, things can head swiftly down a different track. On paper, a career might look like it requires one set of skills, but the culture or demands of the environment might demand another. You might be employed initially for one role but end up placed in a different department, or working on a different project, or relocated to another part of the organization entirely. And – in a particularly odd feature of the typical career hierarchy – getting promoted often means starting to do a different kind of job altogether, one that isn't really related to the job that you excelled at (you know, the one that got you the promotion).

This type of thing happens in corporate law a lot, and I'm sure you can see examples elsewhere, too.

Corporate lawyers are thought of as having a particular set of skills – the ability to analyse, to think critically, to debate and argue. But once you start working in a certain position, as a practising lawyer, it's no longer a straightforward application of your skillset to the job description. Sure, you might be using your critical thinking skills, but (for most lawyers) the role is mostly about understanding a client's demands and responding to whatever those happen to be. And as you move up the hierarchy, getting promoted, if you're lucky, to be a law firm partner, you're using a different skillset altogether. At the top of the legal hierarchy (and this applies, of course, to many other corporate structures), the roles are *management-based*, focused on running a business and organizing people, rather than on the substantive skills of the profession (reading, writing, debating and so on). And so, those who dived into the profession because of their love of the work itself can often be rewarded for their excellence by being moved into a different type of work altogether. From one perspective, then, it might be more rewarding – or, at least, more personally meaningful – to sidestep promotion altogether. But in a culture that rewards the relentless pursuit of progress, it's not an easy choice to make.

This is one of the issues with our working environment – the push towards *more*. More promotions, more projects, more pay rises, more success, more movement. Less time spent figuring out if *more* is actually what we want. In this chapter, we'll be taking a moment to pause – to figure out exactly what you want out of your work, and how you'd like your working life to look. We'll use a couple of main strategies to think about these ideas and then we'll regroup at the end of the chapter to see where we're at. See you there.

Going portfolio

Do you know anyone with a portfolio career? The concept has become increasingly popular in the last few years, with more and more employees rejecting a traditional career hierarchy in favour of a more personal, meaningful, intentionally designed approach. The portfolio career concept is certainly appealing. From the worker's perspective, they're able to explore a multitude of career pathways, leaning towards personal passions and talents and interests. And, as the world moves away from traditional ideas of how we should live and work – our social media feeds opening our eyes to endless possibilities; our cultural narrative telling us that *anything could be possible* – it's easy to see how the portfolio concept could grow in popularity in the years to come. But where does this concept come from? And what does it actually look like in practice? (As you can imagine, the answers to that last question are varied and diverse.) We'll take both questions in turn.

The term 'portfolio career' was popularised by an author and philosopher called Charles Handy. In his book *The Age of Unreason* (1989), he describes the concept: 'a portfolio of activities – some we do for money, some for interest, some for pleasure, some for a cause [...] the different bits fit together to form a balanced whole [...] greater than the parts.'[1]

Charles Handy's work was set in the context of changing employment trends and ideals. He recognized that members of the 'portfolio life' were those who wanted more than one project, role or passion at a time, perhaps also working for multiple clients in the process. At its most basic description, this is, essentially, self-employment – a concept we're all familiar with. But the portfolio idea goes deeper. 'Going portfolio' can be about expanding the scope of your work to include all the things you feel reflect your character, or that serve your passions in some way. A portfolio career can fill the gaps that you've been hoping to fill as you search for meaningful work – and allow you to continue paying rent at the same time. A portfolio career is flexible: you can pick and choose, bringing in some elements and discarding others, avoiding clients or tasks or projects you don't want to take on, and diverting your energy towards the things that excite you. It's not *easy*, of course – in exchange for the freedom, you give up the stability, job security and professional community that come with traditional employment. But, if you've done your personal calculation and worked out that the benefits outweigh the negatives, the portfolio route might start to look increasingly attractive.

So, how should you actually create a portfolio career? And is it possible to bring the portfolio element into a full-time job, or is it reserved for those with self-employment status, or with enough financial stability to justify taking the risk? We'll look briefly at both options: first, the portfolio career for a full-time employee (in other words, an individual who works a full-time job *and* seeks a personal portfolio of projects), and second, the portfolio career for a self-employed worker.

A full-time job, plus a personal portfolio

I knew I wanted to be a lawyer early on in life. I'd watched my parents and their own career changes (from musicians to music teachers), and I was looking for something with a clearer professional path – and, frankly, something that provided more long-term stability. I was naturally drawn to law – I loved working with language, shaping and forming words to construct an argument or debate a case. And I wanted a traditional route: studying a subject at university, taking a few years to train, and then qualifying with a certification that allowed me to take the career forwards. It seemed predictable. Secure. Safe. And it *was* all of those things. But what it lacked, in the end, was the depth and range that my other interests – gathered over years of exploration and curiosity – seemed to offer. Going into law (and especially corporate law) demands *all* of you, to a level that I wasn't, at that time, focused enough to give. I could see the path ahead, and it was both exactly what I had wanted, in some ways, and also not what I wanted at all, in others. And with this came a form of guilt: guilt for getting the career path I'd aimed for and not appreciating it fully; guilt for not living up to the expectations of my younger self; guilt for not throwing myself fully into a career that I could have excelled at, if I'd had the genuine passion to accompany the skillset. But the guilt was outweighed by another fear, and that was the fear of staying stuck in a single-direction career path, while also carrying the regret of not having explored other things, or of not having pursued other interests in the way that I knew could be possible.

Eventually, as you'll have guessed from reading this book, I ended up leaving my role as a lawyer. But before that, I took steps to integrate the different aspects of my interests *into* my full-time position as an employee. I was, for a number of years, a full-time worker with a portfolio of other interests. This is a difficult, demanding thing to do – both because of the amount of energy it requires and because of the difficulty of boundaries, priorities and loyalty to various parts of your life. But it *is* possible, and it can form a helpful period of exploration, enabling you to keep your interests and passions close while you also work on figuring out which direction to go. Here are a few lessons I learned along the way.

Design your portfolio in such a way that it feels – at least to you – consistent

Alongside law, my main interests at the time were writing (articles, books), teaching (helping to mentor others, or teaching workshops and classes) and wellbeing (the yoga, Pilates, meditation and movement stuff we've covered in other chapters). To make the 'portfolio' idea work, it was important that these things were brought into my life in a way that complemented my daily work as a lawyer. And so, when I wrote, it was for legal publications, or for the firm I worked for (eventually, I wrote a book for junior lawyers, which – admittedly – might not sound too exciting, but was actually a great way to bring together all sides of my work and interests). When I was teaching or mentoring, it was for aspiring junior lawyers, or at legal conferences, or for new recruits at the firm I worked for. And with the wellbeing side, I brought that into my legal life as well: I taught meditation for lawyers, and yoga classes at the office. This might sound a little forced, or, to put it bluntly, exhausting (looking back, I often wonder where I got the energy) – but the general idea can be helpful. If you have an interest that lies outside of your full-time job, think about ways in which you could integrate the two. If you love to teach people about your passion project, could you host a workshop in the workplace? If you offer a service or skill outside of your day job, can you find a way to link it back to your professional role? It doesn't have to be about bringing your 'full personal self' into the workplace, either. This is more of a practical step, enabling you to expand your portfolio without spending too much effort trying to separate every aspect of your life.

Let your interests be seasonal instead of evergreen

In this section, we're not talking about adopting new interests every time the seasons change (although, if that works for you, go for it). Instead, we're thinking about 'seasons' in a more metaphorical sense: the seasons of your personal and professional lives. The point is, simply, that you don't have to do everything at once. (This might sound obvious, but we often need to hear it.) The biggest question I get, when talking to people about my portfolio career, is this: how do you have the time to do all of it? Aside from the point that, practically, it builds up over years and years, there's a more basic answer. I don't do everything at once. (I don't even try to.) There hasn't been a single day when I've woken up with a to-do list that involves ticking off every interest, project, professional role and personal commitment on my list. Things come and go in seasons, as with pretty much everything else in life.

In short, you don't have to be an everyday user of a skill or interest for it to have a meaningful place in your portfolio. People may know me as a yoga teacher, but – at least at the time of writing – I don't teach that much yoga. In more recent years, my teaching has shifted away from yoga and towards other disciplines, like Pilates or dance. But people still assume it forms part of my portfolio, and they're right: I still have the qualifications, still have the experience, still have the appreciation for the practice, and still teach occasionally. It's one of the things I'd still include as part of my portfolio of skills. But it's not something I practise or teach every single day. It's not an evergreen portfolio practice; it's seasonal. Or, in other words, you don't have to do it all at once.

Don't assume your portfolio interests should be dropped when other things take up your energy or attention

One of the keys to maintaining a portfolio career while also being in full-time work is to be clear and focused about your priorities. As a full-time employee, your full-time job should come first (if you don't feel that's the case, it might be worth switching into a self-employed option, or at least re-evaluating your choices). This allocation of priorities actually makes your portfolio life easier, in many respects. If you make a commitment to one of your portfolio interests (perhaps you're studying for another qualification after work, or teaching a class at the weekend, or writing a blog on a topic of interest during your lunch break) and your full-time job makes reasonable demands on your time, you know which one comes first. You can also set some clear boundaries for yourself, like not working on your portfolio interests while you're focused on your full-time career (and vice versa).

However, it's important that your list of priorities remains just that: a *list*. There are things higher on the list and lower on the list. The things that get pushed down the list as other elements take priority don't necessarily fall off forever. For example, just because you have a focused and high-energy period at your full-time job doesn't mean it's worth giving up on your other interests entirely. If you're exhausted, make space for yourself. It doesn't mean you've failed to keep your portfolio alive. There's a quote that sums up this principle (often attributed to the artist Banksy, although the origin is unknown), that reads: *'If you get tired, learn to rest, not to quit.'* That kind of idea is helpful to keep in mind as a portfolio creator, because you're signing up for a lifestyle that will probably, at some point, make you tired. The skill to cultivate is the ability to rest, recover, and then steadily, with intention, take the next best step forward.

A full-time portfolio career

After I left law, it appeared as if I had a range of options. Without the commitment of a full-time job, the path seemed fairly open for me to choose what I wanted to do next. This sounds exciting, but – when faced with all the possibilities, plus various financial constraints – it can also be exhausting, draining and intimidating. What happens if you try something that doesn't work out? What if everyone is watching to see what you do next, and you make a mistake, or regret your decision, or get into financial difficulty and have to quickly find another job? The fear of taking the wrong step can be paralyzing.

And, fundamentally, to even have the chance to 'go portfolio' to begin with can be an immense privilege, depending on the circumstances. Many of us were raised by parents and grandparents who would have considered such a move to be a reckless or risky career strategy. But even the privilege comes with its own challenges. What happens when you don't live up to expectations? What if you have this moment of privilege and *still* feel like you ended up making the wrong choices, or didn't utilize your opportunities enough, or – when it comes down to it – what if it simply feels like it's all too difficult to make it work?

The self-employment route can also be lonely, especially if you're swapping out a strong community of co-workers in favour of going it alone. The lack of accountability alone can be overwhelming, and, on top of that, there's all the more subtle stuff: no colleagues to share experiences and opinions with; no casual chats around the coffee machine; no mentoring or professional reviews, and no one telling you if you're doing a good job or not. Maybe you don't think you'll miss all this stuff (I certainly didn't). But it impacts you in less obvious ways, and it develops over time. Without a self-imposed support system, or a way of communicating with others about your professional development, you can easily fall into isolation. With all that in mind, here are a couple of thoughts and learnings I gathered from the move into my own self-employment portfolio life.

Be easy on yourself during the transition

My final day in my full-time job was a Friday, at the end of the month. I'd thought, somewhat naively, that Friday would be for finishing everything off, the weekend would be for a short break, and Monday would be the day to kickstart a new life of freedom. As you can imagine, things didn't quite work out the way I'd hoped. What felt effortless in my imagination was, when it came down to it, exhausting, disorienting and difficult. My first day as a self-employed worker was far from enjoyable. That feeling of meaning, purpose and *aliveness* was pretty far from my mind (instead, I was wondering whether I should get another full-time job as soon as possible). The vast majority of us face the same hurdles when it comes to big personal or professional changes: self-doubt, a fear of failure, and insecurities about whether or not we'll actually be able to do whatever it was we set out to do. And I haven't found a quick fix to any of this either (just in case you've skim-read down to find the solution). But I do think it helps, on some level, to both *expect* and *embrace* this feeling – of stepping out into the unknown. And, on a personal level, I also found it helpful to release some of the pressure of getting it right on day one. We love to rush, in a world that pushes us faster and faster towards an invisible finish line. But what would happen if you resisted the pressure, and paused instead? Took your time with the change? Rested a little along the way? After all, you're building the architecture of your life – it's worth paying as much attention as you can.

It's OK to incorporate a variety of portfolio elements (and some that you prefer over others)

Some people (myself included) can get wrapped up in the ideals of a portfolio life. Waking up on your own schedule, going for a leisurely walk in the morning, taking your time with your work and – fundamentally – doing the things you love most for the entirety of your day. There's nothing wrong with having ideals, of course, and it's always a helpful exercise to map out for yourself what your dream portfolio life would look like. But, as with all vision boards and hopes for the future, the reality is likely to feel a little more mundane. Portfolio workers might eventually reach a time where their working schedule aligns perfectly with the desires and preferences of each day, but, realistically, most of us will take some time to get there. To begin with, your portfolio career needs to work on a very practical level, which usually means you'll be dividing your time between passion projects and projects that keep paying your bills.

Charles Handy (the creator of the modern 'portfolio' concept[2]) thought of his own work in four main 'chunks': paid work, study work, gift work and home work. He saw each of them as requiring an allocation of time, in order to have a fully balanced life. And the first category was simple: paid work. Handy used a central guiding question: *How much income is necessary to meet my needs?* After making the calculation, he could work out exactly how much time to allocate to paid work and what rate to charge his work at. Next, study work was about ongoing professional development – keeping himself up to date with the skills that formed the foundation of his portfolio. Gift work was the idea of service, of giving something back (much more on that topic later). And home work was the responsibility for managing and upkeeping a personal life. That last one might seem a little outdated, but the principle remains: part of your portfolio is care for your personal life, for yourself and your home responsibilities, whatever they might look like for you.

All this is to say, your portfolio will look different from everyone else's, and it might include elements that you're eventually hoping to phase out. That's OK: in fact, it's part of the creation process. With a portfolio career, we're constantly re-evaluating, re-creating – checking to see which elements we want to prioritize and which elements we hope to leave behind. The beauty of the portfolio idea is that it actually *allows for*, and is *designed to support*, this kind of creative flexibility. Unlike full-time work, you don't have to stick to a particular path. You get to choose how to shape your portfolio over time, even if it does include things you choose out of necessity rather than personal preference.

Use comparison as an intentional tool, for your advantage

The portfolio path is increasingly widespread, but it's also entirely individual. Each person's portfolio is a reflection of the elements they've brought together: a wholly unique crafting of a personal and professional life. But even long-term portfolio creators can succumb to the risk of comparison. In a culture that constantly measures us against one another, and with the backdrop of social media and its filtered glimpses of false realities, it can be difficult to stay focused on our own next steps. But it's worth noting that comparison *does* have a role in some circumstances. Think about a typical employee performance review process for a professional business. Within that kind of process, you're not held to imaginary or individual standards, at least when it comes to measuring the merit of your work. You're held to the standards of the average (or above-average) employee. And that, in itself, is an act of comparison, even if you're not being compared against a specific human being. So, when it comes to the portfolio career concept, there's a balance to be found between discarding all comparison in order to go your own way, and, on the other hand, losing the sense of personal and professional comparison that guides you to improve, work better and level up. You don't want to lose yourself in someone else's goals, but you *also* don't want to lose motivation for your own goals, or settle into complacency when you know you could go for more.

One of the best strategies, in this respect, is to set your goals at regular periods (quarterly, or every few months) and then get your head down in pursuit of them. This kind of focus enables you to keep moving forwards, but you move towards the goals that *you* set for yourself. You don't keep peering up and looking around to see what others are doing – you set your goals with the context in mind, taking into account all the achievements you admire in your peers and among your network, and then you just go for it. This kind of practice takes patience, energy and commitment, but it works in your favour over time. As much as you need to invest in the process, you'll gain back far more in peace of mind, a feeling of self-assurance and a sense of personal development, according to your own standards. Easier said than done, but it's certainly worth trying.

EXERCISE 1

Designing your portfolio

In this exercise, we'll dive a little deeper into the mechanics of the portfolio life itself. This is an exercise for *both* of the port-folio types we explored above: the full-time portfolio worker (in other words, you have a full-time role, but with elements of other projects and pursuits) and the self-employed portfolio designer (in other words, your full time career is comprised of 'portfolio-style' projects and positions). And this exercise is also applicable throughout your portfolio-creation journey. It can form a very early step (giving you some ideas for where to start), but it can also become an exercise that accompanies you over time (as we've discovered, the task of crafting a port-folio is an ongoing one). Here's how to get started.

1. Make a long list of all of your skills, abilities and talents. Be generous with the scope of the list: include everything you can think of, work-related or otherwise. If it feels uncomforta-ble to be listing out your skills, you can complete this exercise from a third-person perspective, as if you were an outsider making an objective assessment. Use any feedback you've received in the past to guide you, or any positive responses you've had to your past work or initiatives.

To help you kickstart the process, consider the following questions:

- What skills or talents are you known for, either among your friends or among your professional network?

- Was there anything you were particularly good at as a child? Anything people would have remembered you for?

- Do you have any key passions, interests or pursuits? Think, in particular, of the things you love doing *so much* that you wouldn't mind if you were bad at them. In other words, what are the things that you're willing to dedicate time to because of the joy within the activity itself, rather than the outcome?

- Which parts of your life would you continue pursuing if you had no financial pressure? Which parts would you continue pursuing if you had no social pressure (in other words, if no one was looking)?

- Complete the following sentence using a description of your professional identity: *my name is [X], and my main professional focus is [Y]*. After you complete the sentence using your current role and position, reconsider it from a purely hypothetical position. How would you change it, if you could? Ideally, what would you like it to say?

2. Go back through the steps above and gather all of the findings. Pick out key words, phrases and indicators – perhaps highlight or underline them in a different colour, if it helps. See if you can spot consistencies, themes or general principles

emerging. If you were to select three elements to comprise your portfolio career, which ones would you keep? Which ones would you leave behind?

3. Once you have some general themes or ideas, get even more specific. Map out an ideal 'day in the life' of your portfolio career. Be intentional and precise with the details. What time does your day start? What's the first activity you do? Do you spend your day at your desk, or elsewhere? When do you take breaks, and what do you do with them? When do you finish your day, and is there anything you schedule into your personal time afterwards? This step uses the building blocks of your portfolio skills and abilities, and shapes them into an idealistic version of reality. You can rerun this step as many times as you want, shifting parts around and redesigning until you get an idea of the typical day you'd like to have. Without straying too far into the territory of vision boards and manifestation, the purpose of this step is to get a sense of *what*, exactly, you want.

4. Using all the materials and suggestions from the steps above, map out your central, current portfolio elements: practical skills, talents, abilities and interests that you can include today. You don't need to think immediately about how to make money from it, either – your portfolio might start off with a collection of skills you'll work on or study over time and only turn into streams of income later. For now, just pick out the main blocks you'd like for the foundation of your portfolio and note them down somewhere. We'll return to this idea – and the practical steps that follow as you create your portfolio – later in this chapter.

Meaningful work

Let's step back from the portfolio concept and head a little deeper into the *meaning* that work can deliver to us, portfolio careers or not.

Here, it can help to distinguish 'meaning' from 'purpose'. When we talk about 'finding purpose', we're usually talking about something a bit more practical. Purpose-finding is typically the task of discovering the reasons and motivations behind the work that we undertake and the choices we make. This type of work is closely related to goals, ambitions and action. It's fascinating work, of course, but it's a little different from the work of this book, which is more closely aligned to the topic of *meaning*. We could, in summary form, say that purpose-finding work is the surface level (think: finding your practical reason for getting up in the morning) and meaning-focused work takes us one level deeper (think: finding or shaping your philosophy of life).

Purpose-finding is the type of task you're doing when you work through a concept like *ikigai* (the Japanese technique used to map out your strengths, preferences, monetization strategies and your acts of service to the world).[3] Purpose-finding grounds itself in reality, helping you figure out what you're going to do with your time. But meaning-focused work has a slightly different approach. Meaning-focused work doesn't necessarily need to achieve anything; it doesn't need to result in a plan or a new set of goals. Instead, meaning-focused work is closely aligned with the topic of *values*, of what really matters to you.

Viktor Frankl, and others in the field of logotherapy, had plenty to say about work, and life, and how the two interact. One of his central warnings, when it came to the creation of a meaningful life, was the risk of work priorities overtaking the importance of life itself. As anyone who has worked a demanding job will know, this is a very real possibility – and perhaps even more so now, in a hyperconnected, globalized world. I'm sure I'm not alone in feeling the temptation to check my email during holidays, family events or other meaningful occasions. It's hard to stop, even when you get the chance to do so. (One of my most memorable experiences of my monastic experience was sitting on the floor of a monastery, hoping (praying?) for my phone to get *just enough* signal so I could email my boss back. Needless to say, this wasn't particularly useful for my spiritual growth, or for my pursuit of a meaningful life.)

Speaking about the manager or executive whose work overcame all other aspects of their life, Frankl noted that, for them, 'livelihood overshadowed life' – a slightly jarring phrase (and one that might make us reconsider our promotion ambitions).[4] We can all think of a couple of people who fit this description. Maybe you're even thinking of yourself.

So, what could we be doing to rescue ourselves from this scenario? Not many of us are fortunate enough to find jobs that we love and – if we're not interested or able to pursue the portfolio-style option – what happens if we have to keep trudging down an unsatisfying career path until retirement? In the following sections, we'll explore a couple of strategies, drawn from existential methods, that might help us reorient ourselves towards a sense of meaning in whatever work we do (or even if we're not currently undertaking a 'traditional' form of work at all).

1. SERVICE

This is an idea we'll return to in the next chapter, but for now it's worth mentioning: *service* is nearly always a helpful stepping stone to finding meaning.

Let's imagine you work a desk job – perhaps from home – with limited interaction with your colleagues. Perhaps you have a repetitive, organized task (for example, document review) that takes up most of your working hours. And let's assume you're not involved in the final output of the work – perhaps your work gets passed up the hierarchy, until the boss sends it out to the client, who uses it for their own purposes in the world. Finally, let's assume those purposes aren't connected to a direct social impact – in other words, you're not working for a charity or other type of social enterprise. Where can you find meaning in this kind of job? (This, by the way, isn't too far from the job of a junior corporate lawyer – which is why this example has a personal resonance for me.)

A central guiding question to help you, during this period of meaning-orientation, is this: *Whom do I serve during the course of my work?* If it's obvious, an immediate answer might come to mind, but if it's more complex, as it is for so many of us, it's worth writing down a few notes. List all the people your work has an impact on, both directly and indirectly. Make your list expansive: include everyone you have some type of interaction with, where that interaction serves a purpose – for example, where it helps someone with their work, makes a work product better, makes a system more efficient, improves someone else's day, and so on. If you mentor junior colleagues or other members of your network, include that. If you help to improve the quality of someone else's work, include that. If your work isn't really related to any of these scenarios, just track through every moment of a typical day, asking yourself: *How does my work put something back into the world, something of value?*

Completing this exercise may not pave a clear path towards finding meaning, but it's certainly a revealing process. At the very least, you discover whether or not you have an element of 'service' (or, more basically, helping others or giving back) in your job, and, if you do, whether this element is really enough to sustain you. It's important to bear in mind, though, that discovering there is a lack of service in your job doesn't have to point you directly towards handing in your resignation. It might just indicate that you could search for, and integrate, an element of service elsewhere in your life. More on that in the next chapter.

2. RELATIONSHIPS

Building from the theme of service, it's clear that our relationships can also offer a sense of meaning – including those at work. For this category, note down the relationships with any of your work colleagues or broader professional network that have been meaningful to you. Include the reasons *why* those relationships have been meaningful. The meaningful moment could be as fleeting as a brief piece of advice passed down to you from a senior co-worker, or a time where you supported another member of your network or a colleague with a project or ambition. What, exactly, was it that gave those relationships depth? Again, be generous with the scope of the exercise. You don't need to have formed lifelong bonds with someone in order to find an element of meaning in your relationship.

Under this section, you can also include the times you created new relationships out of a shared professional goal. Recall the times where you worked together with someone else to achieve an ambition or meet a deadline for a client or customer. In the process of collaboration and mutual support, we often find an element of relationship, whether you noticed it at the time or not. And within this relationship, we can often find a sense of meaning.

3. YOUR LIFE PLAN

Sometimes, we have goals that stretch way out into the future. We want to pay off our student debt, or save for a mortgage deposit, or, eventually, leave our city and move out somewhere else. Maybe we want a quieter pace of life or a faster one. Maybe we want a significant career pivot and we hope to end up doing something else entirely. These types of future goals are fantastic motivators, and they can give us the energy to get up in the morning and keep going. Often, though, they take a long time to come into being – and in the meantime, we still have to pay bills, uphold responsibilities and continue to grow, both personally and professionally. So, we might end up putting our dreams on hold in order to keep ourselves going, with the intention that we'll *one day* get around to achieving our ambitions. It might sound like this isn't a particularly meaningful course of events. But, in fact, this is a scenario full of meaning. Far from being a distraction from our goals, or a barrier in the way of our ambitions, we can see our current circumstances as the first step on the road. The dream job (or life, or house, or salary, or anything else) is still out there, waiting in the future to be brought into reality. But if our current situation requires us to work an unfulfilling job, we don't have to choose between a meaningful life or a meaningless one. We can find a sense of meaning among the *current* framework of our life, whatever it might look like. We can see it as providing the starting point for whatever comes next.

It's worth mentioning, here, that I'm not advocating for a positive mindset as a substitute for real change. I don't think, for example, that hoping or planning or dreaming is a replacement for initiating the practical steps you need to take towards your goal. But that's not what this section is about. Instead, you're blending two things together: the hope of a meaningful future *and* the meaning that can be found in the current moment as you work towards that future. You don't always have to pick. Your life is spacious enough to include *both*.

Designing your job

In the final section of this chapter, we're going to be tying together the work we've done so far and then looking onwards to set ourselves a few practical steps. The purpose of the book, and of this chapter, is to find and connect with a sense of *aliveness*, and we've looked at it from a couple of angles: exercising creative design in the formulation of your own portfolio (if you choose that path), and finding elements of meaning within whatever work you end up doing. The last piece of work we'll do here is intended to bring these two elements together, looking holistically at what it means to have a meaningful, personal career, whatever job title you have. This work applies if you're a student, or on a gap year, or on a career break, or retired, or part-time. It works if you're the CEO of a multinational corporation, or if you have a nine to five job that you complete from your bedroom. As with most of the practices in this book, it's not so much about *external appearances* when it comes to pursuing a personal sense of aliveness. It's about depth, experience, and how it actually feels to live your life, on a day-to-day level.

In this final section, then, we're going to work through five practical steps you can take to get started in crafting the working life you want to live. Eighty thousand hours of your time, remember? It's worth making them as meaningful as possible.

1. START AND END YOUR WORKING DAY WITH A PERSONAL CHECK-IN

When it comes to the professional world, most of us are answerable to bosses or supervisors or managers. Unless you're the CEO (and, in fact, even CEOs have to answer to directors, investors and stakeholders), it can be difficult to maintain a sense of personal authority. Usually, we get told to execute a task, and we do it. We're often given work according to someone else's schedule, or someone else's perception of our abilities. Somewhere along the way, our own ideas of meaningful work can get bypassed.

There are lots of methods to overcome this loss of personal authority – including some that we've covered in this chapter already. But you can also go right back to basics, with a simple step that helps you reconnect with who you are and what you're doing with your time. If you can take a few minutes at the beginning and end of each day (or, at least, the days where it's possible to fit it into your schedule), create a check-in ritual for yourself. This could be as simple as reminding yourself of your personal purpose, or setting yourself an intention for the day ahead. Or, you could create a short checklist of questions to help you stay focused, grounded and connected to your personal sense of meaning. For example, you could include questions like:

Where can I find a sense of meaning today?
How can I serve others in my work today?
What kind of qualities, attitudes and values will I bring to my relationships with others today?

At the end of the day, you can quickly review your notes, or your intention, and see where you ended up. If you're consistently feeling like your days are veering off into a different direction from your personal sense of meaning and purpose, it might be a helpful indication that it's time to re-evaluate your working life. Again, drawing on the discussion above, no actions – career or otherwise – have to be immediate or permanent. It's simply another piece of feedback in the long, slow process of figuring out where meaning lies for you.

2. INCLUDE AT LEAST ONE MEANINGFUL ACTIVITY, EVERY DAY

Once you settle into the rhythm of daily working life, it's easy to lose sight of what you're working towards and why you're putting so much energy into it (other than for more straightforward financial and practical reasons). One way to keep yourself close to a sense of meaning and work-related purpose is to schedule a single meaningful activity into your working day, to be carried out each and every day. This activity could be as simple as researching or reading into a topic that interests you, or mentoring a junior colleague. It could also be something that takes you outside the work environment – perhaps leaving work on your lunchbreak to get some movement in, or to call someone you love. Other examples include working on projects or initiatives within your daily schedule that feel personally meaningful to you, or on those that stand out from other parts of your job as being especially interesting. Remember: finding a sense of meaning doesn't have to come from realizing huge ambitions or making grand gestures. If a lunchtime walk outside gives you a sense of grounding, connection and peace, you can find meaning there.

3. USE YOUR OWN STRENGTHS TO TAILOR YOUR JOB DESCRIPTION

When it comes to our daily tasks and to-do lists at work, it can feel like we don't have a choice. If we work within a big corporate organization, or if we're directly answerable to a boss or supervisor, we end up doing what we're told and what we're paid to do. We're entitled to leave it at that, of course – work doesn't have to be the primary source of meaning in our lives, and perhaps we just enjoy getting the job done and then swiftly getting out of the office. But for those of us looking to shape and refine the tasks we do at work, the practicalities of doing so are often more available than we think.

The first step in this 'redesign' process is figuring out exactly *what* it is we want to do. As with many meaning-related exercises, the first step can sound unbearably obvious, but it's easy to overlook. What is it we want? What would an ideal, meaningful day look like for us? Can we visualize it? Do we really know, with specificity, what it might include?

Once we've figured that out, the next step is to find small ways – almost imperceptible at first – to bring this personal design into our everyday work. We're playing a long game here: things are unlikely to transform overnight. This type of job shifting requires patience, consistency and – importantly – good relationships with the people who can make it happen for us (our bosses, or our colleagues, or our clients).

Let's say you've decided you have a particular interest in a certain field of work, one that your job *touches on* but doesn't fully encompass. Once you've figured out this desire, think of five small ways you can start to pivot your career in that direction. If it's an area of expertise you want to develop, could you write an article or other resource, educating people on the details? If it's a type of skill you want to progress (for example, public speaking or presentation), could you organize an opportunity to practise it, or put yourself forward for something?

It takes a shorter time than you'd expect to become the 'go-to' person for a particular skill, area of expertise or insight – and *especially* at work, where most people are simply trying to get the job done. If you're intentional, careful and deliberate with your efforts, you can stand out from the crowd with relatively little effort.

One final note about job tailoring. On the other side of this privilege (the privilege to do work that you love) is responsibility. The responsibility is to take your role and position seriously, and to show up for the things you said you wanted. It's always OK to change your mind, but if you actively hold yourself out as a person to rely on, and if you're granted the permission you wanted, you have a corresponding responsibility to give it your best.

4. CREATE SOMETHING NEW: A PROJECT, A MOVEMENT, A COMMUNITY ...

Related to job tailoring is the idea of *creation*, within your working life. When it comes to your daily work routine, it can be hard to see how you can create new things, or innovate existing processes. Things are often done a certain way, especially in the corporate context, and it can feel overwhelming or pointless to try anything new. But it's often not as difficult as it appears. In particular, when it comes to traditional, established ways of doing things, processes are frequently crying out for an innovative reappraisal. Someone who takes the time to step back, look at a situation and suggest a new way of doing things can be an incredibly valuable asset for an organization (not to mention the satisfaction that you, as an individual, can get from the process).

Similarly, creating a new initiative – a community group, a new project, a shared-interest club with your co-workers – is often well received, and can enable you to bring some of your personal sense of meaning and purpose into your daily working life. Creativity is a fundamental aspect of the search for meaning, and it can give us that essential sense of 'forward movement' in our lives. Where are we headed? What will we create? How will we choose to change things in the future? We get to decide.

5. THINK ABOUT YOUR NEXT STEPS IN THE CONTEXT OF A GREATER NARRATIVE

A final note, here – and one that takes us slightly away from the other points in this list. This final point is about seeing your present moment as part of a longer, more integrated narrative: the narrative of your life. If you're working in a corporate job that you dislike, or you're stuck in an industry you don't see a future in, it can be easy to fall into a sense of despair or disappointment. If we can't see the future (or if we don't even know what we *want* our future to look like), things can get bleak pretty quickly.

One possible solution is to see our lives and work in the context of an ongoing narrative. To start to look at ourselves in this way, we first have to do the work of figuring out what we want (by now, this first step might sound familiar!). What are our career dreams? Where do we want to be in five years' time? In ten years? What's the ultimate goal? Get specific, here – not just a vague statement (for example: wanting to be wealthy), but one with details (for example: *I want to earn an annual salary of [insert your dream salary], working in [insert your dream industry]*).

Once you have the ultimate goal, you're going to unravel it: work backwards, weaving a path all the way from that ultimate goal to where you are right now. In other words, you're mapping in reverse – figuring out the hypothetical steps it would take you to get from *here* to *there*. These steps don't have to be exact, and they're not a specific plan to be followed unwaveringly. Instead, they allow you to bring the present moment, with all of its dissatisfactions and annoyances, into the broader picture of your life. Where you are right now is not a mistake. It's the starting point – or, more accurately, a step on the journey to somewhere else. The work you're doing now is helping you get to where you want to be, eventually.

Before we go on

Our work in this chapter has taken a more practical approach: instead of dealing with our personal circumstances (our minds, our bodies), we've been looking externally, at the path we choose to take through the world. But, at the same time, we've been working with consistent principles: autonomy and freedom; a deep connection to the self; a sense of meaning and purpose; an ability to claim creative control. The topic of 'work' might seem a little boring – or stressful – but it doesn't have to be. The work you choose to do, or the way in which you choose to do your work, is as much an exercise of your artistic 'life design' as any of the other practices in this book. And just like the other practices, your work-related choices are always open to be revisited and redesigned, whenever you feel necessary.

CHAPTER 7

Self

. . .

As we head towards the end of our work together, we'll start to focus in on 'the self' – in other words, *you*, at your deepest level. Working with a broad, integrated perspective, we'll move briefly through spirituality, authenticity, boundaries, personal evolution, and our pursuit of meaningful relationships, both with ourselves and with others.

Before we begin

Ever since human history was first recorded, we've been meaning-seeking creatures. Paintings on cave walls, carvings in rock faces, rituals and ceremonies. Dedications. Sacrifices. Religion and tradition and rites. There's something in our species that calls out for *more*: more than this, the material life we currently have. We're looking for depth and dimension to our experience on this earth, and if we can't immediately find it, we create it.

What would it mean, then, if our future is a post-religious world? What happens to our sense of meaning and purpose when there is no longer a spiritual rhythm to our days and weeks, or when every day looks the same? What happens when we don't have sacred spaces, or when churches are converted into supermarkets and yoga studios become just another place to take a selfie?

To be clear, I don't necessarily think the secular evolution of our culture is an entirely bad thing. Religion and spirituality have caused their fair share of conflict in the past, of course. And even as a person with a strong religious practice, I don't think it should be something that ends up imposed on society, just because the opinion of the majority – whoever that happens to be at the time – says it should be. But I do wonder what the long-term implications will be for a culture that drops its sense of spiritual structure. Without a clear divide between spiritual and secular life, what happens? Do we lose a source of meaning? Or perhaps, without religion, everything might become *more* awe-inspiring, *more* extraordinary, simply because it's all so unlikely that we're here, and we're *alive*! After all, what are the chances of that?

This chapter – spoiler alert – doesn't answer any of those questions. But it does work through some central spiritual practices that have been helpful to me, on my own journey, as I've moved through both spiritual and secular worlds. These practices span religion, spirituality, tradition, philosophy and anthropology, and they each have something unique to teach us. The way you choose to integrate them into your life – well, just like the rest of the book, that's up to you.

A ritual of rest

The practice of Sabbath comes from a commandment in the Bible – in the Book of Exodus, to be specific. The commandment reads like this: 'Remember the Sabbath day, to keep it holy.' And then, to follow up: 'Six days you shall labor, and do all your work, but the seventh day is the Sabbath of the LORD your God. In it you shall not do any work.' And, later: 'For in six days the LORD made heaven and earth, the sea, and all that is in them, and rested on the seventh day' (Exodus 20:8–10), with an implied rejoinder: 'So why can't you?'. (Seems like a fair point.)

The word 'Sabbath' itself comes from the Hebrew word *shabbath*, generally meaning 'rest'. In the Jewish faith, the Sabbath is observed on a Saturday. For Christians who follow the practice, it's often observed on a Sunday. The core concept is similar: there should be one day a week that is set apart, made 'holy'. Sabbath can be an immensely powerful practice because, given an enforced opportunity to pause and reflect, we can discover new depths to our own existence. As Oliver Sacks wrote, in an essay for the *New York Times* in 2015:[1]

'The peace of the Sabbath, of a stopped world, a time outside time, was palpable, infused everything, and I found myself drenched with a wistfulness, something akin to nostalgia, wondering what if: What if A and B and C had been different? What sort of person might I have been? What sort of a life might I have lived?'

Another theme, drawn out in this passage, is the idea of a *collective* rest – a period of social and communal Sabbath. The whole world is stopped, not just you, by yourself. You don't typically get called into work in the middle of Sabbath practice. For those of us who didn't grow up with a family or community experience of Sabbath (or similar practice), the closest we've probably come is a quiet bank holiday, or the Christmas/ new year celebration period. But it's not exactly like either of those. It's not a celebration, or a chance to indulge, or to briefly abandon all responsibilities (as much as this might, actually, be what we need every now and then). Instead, Sabbath is an opportunity to go inwards: to listen to yourself, to God (if you're religious), and to your life. To *pause*, before we race back into the week, and to adjust your course, if you notice you've been going off track.

Without taking away from the integrity of Sabbath as a traditional spiritual practice, then, what can we learn from the Sabbath ritual? How can we use some of the wisdom of this ancient spiritual discipline to give our lives greater depth, direction and meaning? I think there are a couple of ways.

First, we can see, within the practice of Sabbath, the importance of *rhythm* and *cycles* to our lives. We're not really designed to be all-on, 24-hour creatures. We need a rise and a fall, an exertion and a reflection, a sprint and a cool-down. We need a rhythm like the Sabbath practice, and yet we live in a society that encourages us to race forwards without stopping. The fascination with hyper-productivity and endless optimization – of our personal lives, as well as of our professional lives – leaves us with an obsession for generation, expansion, performance, delivery and growth. These are all good things, to some extent, but they should form only one component within our lives. The other components should be things like relationships, self-reflection, rest and ... well – Sabbath, or something similar.

Second, we can better understand the power of *community*. Moving together through a ritual is far more powerful, in most cases, than moving through it alone. And Sabbath is often a group practice: it starts together, and the end is marked together. So, if you have close personal relationships, it might be worth exploring Sabbath, or a similar practice, together. Moving in a similar rhythm to those you love can also be an immensely deepening experience, when it comes to the quality of your relationships.

And third, we can better *distinguish* periods of time from one another. If you've ever had the feeling that all the days are the same, or that your whole life is merging into one homogenous blob, then you're not alone. In a secular society, we gain a lot of things, but we lose some as well – and one of the losses is that of sacred time. This, to return to the main Sabbath commandment, is the idea of keeping one day *holy* – set apart, or made different, from the rest. And this is what Sabbath enables us to do – to make a divide between *the first six days* and *the seventh day*, and give that seventh day a special kind of quality: a sacred, or – some would say – a holy quality.

The in-between times

An underground car park. A school corridor during the summer holidays. The moment of birth or of someone passing away. The space of time between finishing one thing and starting another. The few seconds after you hear some news that will change your life.

What do all of these examples have in common? According to a variety of sources, including both academic anthropology and mystical spirituality, we could describe these periods of time, or places, or events, as *liminal space*. Liminal space – from the Latin word *limen*, meaning 'threshold' – is the 'in-between' time or space. It's not quite one thing and not quite the other. When it comes to liminal time, we're often thinking about the gaps between the ending of something and the beginning of something else. Think of the summer breaks between your school years, for example. Sometimes we have such nostalgic, vivid memories of those summer holidays, which seemed to stretch on forever – we have these memories because those moments in time were distinct, different from other periods of time in our lives. We can call these moments *liminal space*.

When it comes to physical places, the idea is similar: liminal spaces often arise when one thing (a school corridor, for example) is seen or experienced out of its normal context (during the summer holidays, to continue the same example). This is disorienting to us because we have strong associations with places and their activities, or their purposes, or their context. When we step into these liminal spaces, we lose our anchor to the present moment, to whatever is actually happening *right now*. We struggle to place ourselves *here*, because our minds or memories or instinctive associations are somewhere else. Liminal spaces can also be found in places that we associate strongly with personal memories. Think of the street on which you grew up, or the house in which you spent your earliest childhood. Think of the houses or cars of ex-partners, or of people who are no longer in your life. Remember the restaurants of first dates, or the routes you used to walk to get to a job you no longer have. These places, with such particular resonance for us, can seem perfectly ordinary to everyone else. A street is just a street, until it isn't 'just a street', because it carries a certain association for us, or because it reminds us of a certain person (or even a former version of ourselves).[2]

One final example of liminality: the example of initiation rituals or rites. As humans, we pass through seasons of life, moving from generation to generation, and our species has long been recorded as having an instinct to mark these transitions with ceremony. The 'coming of age' ceremony, largely still practised across the world (other than in many Western countries, in which the idea has been somewhat diluted into a prom night or graduation), is one of the central examples of liminal ritual. Across some West and Central African countries, a tradition called 'the Mekuyo rite' shows this type of 'threshold' transition:[3] a long performance takes place, including singing, dancing and costumes, after which a participant may be said to enter a new stage of life. Liminal traditions and rituals are, from a psychological perspective, useful in supporting us as we move between stages of life, often guiding our maturity and growth.

On a personal level, you might already be starting to see the ways in which liminal space can be helpful. We could take the grieving process as an example of supportive liminal time: it takes a long period of time to shift fully into the next stage of life after a loss, and liminal space defines this 'in-between' period. It would be strange to wake up the next morning and start a fully new beginning, at least psychologically. Liminal time provides us with space as we find our feet within whatever comes next. As for liminal places, their significance can alert us to something meaningful within ourselves. If a place feels particularly disorienting, or wrapped up in memories, it's a sign that we've attributed that place a certain importance or purpose. This realization, and the acceptance of our liminal experience, can help us figure out what it was we valued about that place, and then we can give it the significance it deserves.

And with regards to liminal ritual, its purpose is clear: it helps us move, with intention and grace, towards a new chapter of life.

From that summary, it seems like liminality is a good thing – something we should actively embrace, observe and pay attention to. But when it comes to the everyday reality of our lives, things – as always – get much more complicated. Often, we don't like being in liminal space. It feels uncomfortable and disorienting. We're not quite sure what's actually happening. And we don't know what might come next, which, for so many of us (including me), is an unsettling feeling.

And then there's the cultural context and the broader social attitudes to collective liminal space. Remember the beginning of the pandemic years, back in early 2020? As we moved through the initial weeks, you could say that – as a whole – society was in transition, experiencing liminality on a global level. We didn't know what was coming next, but we knew, as the weeks went by, that what we'd left behind wasn't necessarily coming back. And the experience was painful. Along with the more obvious loss, grief, fear and uncertainty, most of us were trying to get *out* of liminality. This desire manifested in a variety of ways: wanting to move forwards, to get into a more certain future; wanting to move backwards, to get back to the way things used to be; or wanting to define our current experience, by giving it names and labels (remember 'the new normal'?). Either way, we didn't really want to be stuck in the middle, trapped in a space of liminality where the ending was neither certain nor foreseeable.

Liminal space is challenging because it holds us in transition, without our feet on solid ground. We resist change, or try to deny that it's happening, or pretend that we're already over whatever it was and that we've already moved on. But liminality often catches up with us, and it can sometimes bring us right back into a process we thought we'd skipped over. In the end, there's no fast-track pass to moving through the stages of life, no matter how much money you spend or how many books you read.

What's the relevance, then, of all this – in particular, when it comes to your personal path through the world? Well, a couple of things.

First, the ability to notice your own liminal space can be helpful in bringing structure or form to an uncertain situation. By naming the liminality, and by fully participating in it, we can regain a little stability. Not *control*, since liminal space tends to move at its own speed. But *stability*, or, at least, a sense of being more fully grounded.

Second, liminal space offers an opportunity for us to *learn* something. During liminality, our core values, principles, habits, tendencies, preferences and personality traits are revealed, usually against our best attempts to prevent it. Liminal space can unveil the worst sides of ourselves – the sides that resist personal change, or the sides that react with fear and anger against the way our life is evolving. But on the other side of this challenge is an opportunity: the opportunity to learn something about ourselves, or about the place we are in our lives, or about the way we want things to look in the future. When we pass through liminal space, things tend to get shaken up, which is both unnerving and – strangely – liberating. Without our former structures, we can redesign how we'd like things to look. We can make new decisions, or set new goals, or adopt new preferences. We can leave the old versions of ourselves in former time and space. And, ultimately, liminal space does come to an end. It's an in-between time – which means, by definition, that something comes *next*, and it's up to us to decide what, exactly, that is.

Third, once you've developed the ability to notice and hold your own liminal space, you can do so for others. This insight, or alternative perspective, can be incredibly helpful for those who haven't yet encountered the language to name their own liminal space, or who feel a tendency to rush through their own liminal experiences. Equipped with a deeper understanding of liminality, both on a theoretical and personal level, we might just be able to provide a much-needed anchor to someone else as they venture through their own liminality.

EXERCISE 1

A liminality practice

In this exercise, you'll craft your own liminality practice: something to help you as you navigate periods of change, transformation and uncertainty. Following the general approach taken through this book, we'll cover the basic building blocks together and then you'll be free to shape and form this exercise to fit whatever works best for you.

First, name and capture a current example of **liminal space**. What is it, within your life, that you're currently working through? Is there an aspect in which you feel 'stuck' between one thing and another? A relationship or career event that feels unfinished? A season of life that's ending, or one that's just beginning? Whatever it is, give it language. Grab a piece of paper and make some notes, if it helps – or even speak it out loud. Sometimes, the act of giving words to an intangible experience can be one of the most valuable things you can do.

Second, decide what you'd like the **outcome** of your liminality practice to be. If you're wanting to move definitively from one thing to another (for example, wanting to leave behind a relationship, behaviour or habit), decide how you'd like to move forwards on the other side of your practice – how will things be different? If you're simply feeling a little 'stuck', without a clear resolution or path forward, perhaps you'd like your liminality practice to simply create space for you to reflect, or to give you an opportunity to find a creative solution.

Third, design the **ceremony**. If it's helpful, take inspiration from some of the other liminality ceremonies out there – for example, an induction into a new community, or a graduation ritual. Liminality celebrations often include moments of reflection, periods of silence or music, and (if it feels appropriate to your own liminal practice) an opportunity for gratitude or appreciation.

You can design your liminal practice to be as big or as small as you want, involving others if you find it helpful. And, of course, each time you arrive into a new period of liminal space, you can redesign a new practice.

A reflection on death

So, here we are, in a book centred on full *aliveness*, arriving at the topic of death. Why, you might be wondering, would anyone want to spend their time thinking about death? Out of all the things we could be doing with our short-lived existence, why use our time to contemplate the end of it? Good question. In this section, we'll briefly explore the ancient Stoic practice of death contemplation, and then you're free to figure out whether it's something that works for you (or not).

The Stoic philosophers, who were around in ancient Greece and Rome in the third century bce, held to several general principles in constructing their way of life. You may be familiar with these types of Stoic ideas already: the prioritization of virtue, the control of attitude and response, the 'calmness' with which life's challenges should be met. Less frequently discussed, though, is the attitude towards death. Epictetus, for example, writes:

'What harm is there if you whisper to yourself, at the very moment you are kissing your child, and say, "Tomorrow you will die"? So likewise to your friend, "Tomorrow you will go abroad, or I shall, and we shall never see each other again"?[4]

This might sound a bit extreme. But the idea at the heart of this practice is an acceptance of impermanence, and the ability to face reality head on, in its current form, with all of its difficult and (often) disappointing limitations. The Stoic principle goes something like this: if you remain open to the realities and finalities of life, and actively make space to contemplate and come to terms with it all, you will feel more joy with life as it is for you, right now. In other words, contemplating the end might make us feel more grateful for the present moment.[5]

Admittedly, this isn't for everyone, and if it makes you feel disheartened or unhappy, you can always skip to the next section. But for some of us, this can be – and is intended to be – a beneficial practice, perhaps even a joyful practice. After all, we know that our lives will be over, eventually. So, what does that

SELF

mean for the present moment? Well, it could make it more precious and more meaningful. If we had infinite time in these bodies, on this planet, what would be the point of making each moment count? Since our time is finite, we can not only *accept* finality but *embrace* it as the framework of our lives. The Stoic philosophers frequently drew on nature for inspiration and guidance, and one of the core observations was the endless process of change within the natural environment. Seasons come and go; trees shed their leaves and blossom again. And so it is with our lives. We begin, we live, we participate in the world, and then we go.

In a reformulation of Marcus Aurelius's words:

'You've got to hurry, then. You've got to hurry, not only because death draws nearer every day, but because the power to properly think about things and to understand things often leaves us before we die.'[6]

Yikes. But also – what a gift there is, in this present moment.

EXERCISE 2

A brief meditation on finality

(A disclaimer: meditation on the topic of death is not for everyone, and if you feel a little unsure or apprehensive – or if you're encountering any mental health challenges – you can always skip to the next section.)

Begin by sitting comfortably, in a quiet place. Set yourself a timer – ten or fifteen minutes should work well. Allow yourself to settle, and bring your attention to your breath.

Briefly scan through your body. Take into account every inch of yourself, from the soles of your feet to the crown of your head. Visualize the warmth of your skin, the life and vitality in your muscles. Then, bring your attention to your breath. Describe the sensation of the breath, for yourself: is it warm or cool? Fast or steady? Relaxed or tense? You can also imagine the breath running up and down the full length of your body – not only contained in your chest and lungs but expansive, fuelling and replenishing every part of you.

After focusing on the breath for a few moments, bring to mind the following question: *If I were to die tomorrow, how would I live today?*

You might have a million answers to this – none of which will be wrong (or right). But, for the purposes of your meditation, you're seeking to heighten your current experience of *aliveness* by visualizing the opposite – the end, or the finality of life. What would it feel like if you knew your experience of aliveness was coming to an end tomorrow? What would you do differently?

After spending a few minutes running these questions through your mind, come back to the current-moment awareness of your body. One of the main principles of Stoic death meditation is this: we have no idea when our lifetimes will be up. It could be decades away; it could be tomorrow. The point is, according to this meditation technique, to experience the depths of our lives right now. And death meditation can help us to come back into a position of appreciation and gratitude for our lives – not in a superficial or insincere way, but in a deep, fully embodied, wholehearted way. You can return to this meditation practice as often as feels helpful to you, and incorporate it into your portfolio of meditation exercises in any way that works best.

Bookend practices

My experience with 'bookend practices' comes from my training in a monastic community. As you might imagine, life in a monastery is somewhat predictable. For most monastic communities, days follow a certain shape: wake and sleep at a certain time, perform certain rituals, and follow a pattern that may have been followed for generations. For most of us in the modern world, this sounds restrictive. On the whole, we don't like being told exactly how our lives should look. And we're individuals: we like to control the way our days unfold (in fact, maybe that's the reason you picked up this book). But there's also – somewhat counterintuitively – a type of freedom that can be found within the boundaries of restriction. We started this book by talking about the multitude of choice – remember that story about the overwhelming supermarket experience of modern life? – and we've been moving through a variety of options to cultivate your choices in a way that serves you and the life you want to have. And now we're here: thinking about tapering some of those choices down, in order to find more freedom.

Monastic practices vary in scope and expression, but they tend to share some basic features. One of these features is the morning and evening rituals, which – for the purposes of summarizing here – we can call *bookend practices*, for the way in which they 'bookend' the day. In this section, we'll look specifically at practices influenced by St Ignatius, the founder of a 'contemplative spirituality', now known as Ignatian spirituality. St Ignatius (or, according to his original name, Ignatius Loyola) was a Spanish theologian who formed a religious order known as the Society of Jesus (the Jesuits) in 1539. The main ideas of Ignatian spirituality – formulated *before* the development of the religious order, and not intended only for priests or monastic orders – are captured in the *Spiritual Exercises* (1522–4), a collection of meditations, contemplative practices and prayers, designed to be carried out over the course of four weeks. If this sounds like a sixteenth-century self-help programme to you, you're not wrong. The intention behind the exercises was to make a steady commitment to God, over a structured period of time, using themes as guidance, and ending in a wholehearted confirmation of faith. It should be noted, at this point, that the programme (which is often referred to as a 'retreat in daily life') is not intended to be worked through by an individual alone. Instead, Ignatian spirituality advocates for the exercises to be led by a spiritual director or 'guide', to support the process and suggest further readings or next steps. But for the purposes of this section, we're going to be looking at just one of the practices involved in Ignatian spirituality: 'the examen'.[7]

EXERCISE 3

The examen

The examen, or 'spiritual self-review', is essentially a five-step analysis, helping the practitioner assess the day ahead. The steps are, of course, directed towards connection with God, but we'll look at them from a slightly adapted, secular perspective. This is not to dilute the power of the practice as a religious discipline, but to see if it has something useful to teach us about becoming more fully *alive* (which, for what it's worth, as someone who has worked with this practice both in a monastery and out of it – I think it does).

Before you start, find a quiet place and take a notebook and pen. Close your eyes (or unfocus your gaze) for a few breaths.

Awareness

This first step is about becoming present in the space and 'fully arriving' to your practice. If you already have a regular meditation, mindfulness or contemplation practice, the skills required here will be familiar: focusing on the present moment (or your breath, if you use that as a tool) to gather your attention. If you're trying this for the first time, give yourself a few moments to pause before you begin. Allow your breath to slow down and your body to relax. Listen, gently, to whatever you can hear around you, and imagine letting the sounds wash over you without trying to pay too much attention to them. Do the same with your thoughts: allow them to arrive, notice them and then allow them to fade away. After settling your body and mind in this way for a few moments, you should be ready to begin the next step.

Gratitude

Centuries before gratitude started trending under the hashtag 'blessed', St Ignatius was advocating for a morning gratitude practice. In fact, he thought ingratitude was one of the worst sins imaginable. And so, the spiritual exercises begin with gratitude. You arrive in your morning practice as you are, with all of your complaints, discomfort and irritation. Then, you start with an opening up, an offering of yourself and your day, in gratitude. (For those who need a little extra validation from a scientific lens, studies do generally indicate an association between gratitude practices and improved wellbeing, so there's something worth pursuing here.)[8]

Desires

For this step, ask yourself: *What do I desire from my day today?* In Ignatian spirituality, desire is seen as an indication of your true values – the things you hold most important. Being authentic with yourself at this step can help to give your day increased focus, purpose and direction. It sounds obvious, but it's not dissimilar – at least in this regard – to other intention-setting practices, or even to more practical exercises like goal-setting. The most important element here is that you're honest with yourself about what you want. It's possible that this process – of simply and honestly figuring out what you want from your day – will reveal much more than you were expecting.

If you're undertaking a morning 'examen' over a long period of time, you could also consider making a few notes on the process. In particular, when it comes to the topic of desire, watching the evolution of your own preferences and hopes over a period of time can be insightful. Often, our true desires are trapped far beneath the surface and it's difficult to disentangle them from our more immediate desires (for material things, or for quick-fix satisfaction), or from what everyone else seems to want. The process of uncovering your daily desires as part of this exercise might be slow, and it may take weeks, months or years to come closer to what you *really* want, but this everyday discipline is a great way to get started.

Feelings

Often bound up with desires, the next step is to consider your feelings. If the word 'feelings' sounds a bit too intangible, you can substitute this word for emotions, energy, motivation or sensations. In this step, take a broad and holistic view of how you feel. Include your physical sensations – whether you feel tired or energetic, alert or lethargic – as well as your mental state and mood. If it's difficult to pinpoint exactly what it is you're feeling, or if you don't particularly want to unravel the complexity of your feelings on the morning of your practice, you can simply ask yourself: *How did I sleep last night?* A physical-focused question like this, grounded in reality, can often form the starting point for a deeper, more direct assessment of what you're feeling.

The day ahead

Using the findings from your 'desires' and 'feelings' practice, consider the day ahead. What kind of challenges will you face? How do you intend to handle them? What meaningful activities will you add into your day? Where will you find moments of time for yourself, if possible? How can you redirect the course of your day more closely to your personal values and ambitions?

In the Ignatian tradition, this step involves aligning your talents, abilities and gifts with your spiritual path – in other words, focusing on using your day for a greater purpose. If you wanted to add in that element, either from a spiritual perspective or from a broader 'meaning-focused' perspective, you can ask yourself: *How will I use my energy today to create something of value or give something back?*

Starting your day

Once you've finished your five-step practice, take a few
moments to collect your thoughts. The practice can be as long
or as short as you like – and it's wholly possible to do it on the
move (for example, on your morning commute). As a rough
guide, a typical practice could take around ten to fifteen minutes. As with most contemplative disciplines, the important
element is generally the *consistency* of practice, and the *intention* that you bring to the practice itself. So, be experimental:
figure out what works for you and where the practice fits
into your daily timetable. If you take notes, you can review
them every so often – perhaps every few weeks – to observe
the evolution and development of your thoughts. Or, you
might simply prefer to allow the practices to be a personal,
unrecorded commitment. Again, experiment: use the basic
framework as a navigation tool, and craft something that feels
authentic, meaningful and – ultimately – useful to your life.

EXERCISE 4

A closing practice

The end of every day is another great opportunity to form
a meaningful, mindful ritual for yourself. In most monastic traditions, the day ends with 'evening prayer' – or, in
the Benedictine tradition, *compline*. The word 'compline'
comes from the Latin word *completorium*, and the traditional practice of compline was intended to 'complete'
the day. In many Western monasteries, it's customary to

observe silence (sometimes known as the 'Great Silence') until the next day.

For you, trying this practice in the context of your life, it might not be necessary to maintain total silence for the rest of the evening. But there are other ways of bringing stillness and peace to your night – perhaps, after your evening contemplative practice, you put your phone down for the night, or you exit your work emails. Compline, or a more general contemplative evening practice, is a sign that the work of the day is complete. It marks a clear division (there's that 'bookend' idea again) between one day and the next.

In the Benedictine monastic tradition (one of the most well-known Western monastic traditions), compline begins with a brief review of the day. In particular, there's an opportunity to focus on things that *didn't* go so well – challenges, difficulties or struggles faced during the course of the day. The intention of this, though, is not to ruminate on 'sins' or failings but rather to make peace with anything left unresolved. According to St Benedict, the key is to put to rest any anger or resentment from the day and pave the way for a clean slate the next morning. The prayer, then, is for protection, hope and resolution. The practice usually takes place in a dimly lit room, to symbolically close the day, and ends with a blessing.

As with the Ignatian practices we explored above, you don't have to be a Benedictine monk in order to see the value in practices like this. For the religious or spiritual among us, these practices can be structured with God as the main purpose, or as the centre of the ritual. But outside of that context, we can draw on the elements of the discipline for wisdom, teaching and guidance, as we go about structuring our own lives to deliver more meaning and fullness.

CREATING YOUR EVENING PRACTICE

The following elements are usually considered important foundations for an evening practice:

- quiet, or silence
- low lighting
- time and space alone
- reflection and 'resetting'
- intention-setting.

We'll briefly run through these in turn, and the invitation – for you, the creator – is to use the building blocks to design your own practice.

Quiet, or silence

Back to the 'Great Silence' idea that we covered above. This element is considered fundamental, because it provides an effective 'reset' ahead of a new day and an opportunity to mark the closure of the previous day. We often observe silence at meaningful moments – think of the silence used for remembrance events, or the quiet moments scheduled into meaningful celebrations like weddings or ceremonies. Silence can be used to build tension, to show respect, or to simply divide one period of time (the silent period) from another (the rest of life).

For your own evening ritual, consider how you could bring in an element of silence. You don't have to make it a strict rule: think of it more as a guiding principle. It might be that you only say things that are 'necessary' for the rest of the evening, or that you aim to talk only for meaningful conversations, as much as possible. You could also consider using the silence as an opportunity to pause and reconsider what you really want to say to others – maybe your final words of the day, then, become more considered, reflective and personal.

Low lighting

For this element, you could consider lighting candles, or turning down (or off) the lights in your house. If you live with others – who may not be fully aware of your closing practice – think about small steps to take: lowering the brightness on your phone, closing curtains or blinds, or moving to an area with softer lighting. You can also use this element as a reminder to turn off your phone (or, let's be honest, put it on airplane mode or silent) for the rest of the night, if you can. A switch in your visual environment can be a great way to transition from the end of the day to the start of your closing practice.

Time and space alone

For many of us, this might not sound possible – if we live with others, or if we have caring responsibilities, or if we have partners or friends or family that are returning from a day's work and expect us to be fully present with them. In general, it's probably not worth sacrificing your personal relationships with others (and the depth and fullness these can bring) in favour of a strict personal practice – unless you've weighed up the benefits for you, as an individual, and decided that it is, in fact, what you need. Having said that, your closing practice doesn't need to be longer than a few minutes. Think about whether there's anything else you could switch out – a few extra minutes watching Netflix, for example, or a couple of minutes scrolling through social media. And you don't need to keep a strict monastic-style regime in order to find some benefit from a consistent closing practice. Think about cultivating a steady practice over months, rather than days. The long term, when it comes to self-focused routines, is almost always the best outlook to adopt.

Reflection and 'resetting'

Just like the morning 'examen' practice, this step (and the following step) gives you an opportunity to look backwards, at what happened during your day, and then forwards, to the day ahead (on which, see below).

Your reflective practice could be as simple as taking a few moments to scan through your day, noting the challenges and successes, and reminding yourself of anything you would have done differently. Just as for the meditation-based practices we explored earlier in the book, a fundamental component of this practice is *non-judgement*. It's crucial to be able to take an impartial perspective, because judgement and self-criticism aren't actually that productive when it comes to the spiritual path. It might *feel* like it's a helpful process, to criticize ourselves for the things we wish we'd done differently, but it often doesn't get us anywhere. A more useful attitude is to see ourselves from a distance, as human beings trying our best to get through the world, and make changes based on the things that could help us move forwards.

(As a side note, I often get asked for advice on sustaining motivation, energy and determination over a long period of time. There are lots of answers, of course, many that we've explored during the work of this book. But – from my personal experience – one of the central attitudes I have towards myself, probably delivered by a background of psychotherapy and monastic training, is that I try not to be too harsh with myself when it comes to self-development. I make mistakes, sometimes notice them, attempt to fix them, and try to do so in a way that creates something *better* out of the situation, or gives me an opportunity to discover something about myself. This, by the way, is certainly not my natural instinct (which is probably a lot more self-critical). This is a learned behaviour, one that I've been practising over the last decade. And it's one that you can choose and cultivate for yourself, if you feel it would be helpful.)

Intention-setting

In this final step, you'll look ahead. Based on your review of the day, and your current attitude, feelings, awareness and motivation, what do you want to do with your time tomorrow? One relevant idea, central to many theological traditions, is that of *resurrection*. At its core, the concept of resurrection is about leaving the old behind and arising to something new each day. This idea shows up in Western monastic traditions through the closing practice – ending one day completely so that space arises in which to create something new – but it can be found in a variety of other places, including the existential teachings we covered earlier. Viktor Frankl himself, writing about his own experiences of the 'new start' concept, said: 'Live as if you were already living for the second time, and as if you had acted wrongly the first time!'[9] It might sound a bit extreme, but the idea has similar roots:

days come, and they pass, and our lives move onwards. Each morning, we get faced with another opportunity to 'begin again', should we choose to take it.

While spiritual teachings might see this as a daily 'resurrection', you can use the same idea to set an intention for the following day. The intention can be as simple as something like: 'I will be more present and mindful with my time', or a more complex statement relating to a specific goal or ambition. You can formulate intentions around other people as well – relationships are a great context in which to formulate an intention. And one of the most powerful things about intention-setting is the flexibility it brings. It's not a task list for your upcoming day. There's no measurement at the end and no reward for achievement. It's simply a way to reorientate your perspective and energy towards the things that, upon a moment of deeper reflection, you decide that you want.

After you finish

Once the practice is over, be gentle with the rest of your evening. Move slowly, with mindful awareness, if you can. Try not to spike your energy again before the morning. If life gets in the way between your closing practice and sleep, you can give yourself a final reset before bed, if you like. Resting your eyes for a few moments, reconnecting with your breath, feeling a sense of gratitude for your own aliveness, and setting a quick intention for the morning: even a few minutes practising these steps is worth your time.

The rule of life

In this final practice, we'll be looking at something called 'the rule of life'. This is another practice with its roots in monastic community, and it's something that became central to my experience of monastic life. In my own monastic community, the 'rule of life' was a statement of values and principles that we, as members of a community, made a commitment to. The 'rule of life' title might actually be a little misleading, since it wasn't a strict 'rule' (in the sense that breaking it would have negative consequences). Instead, it was more of an aspirational collection of overarching values that we agreed, as a community, to organize our lives around.

Here are a few examples from our rule of life:

- **Silence:** we agreed to make space for silence within our year in the community, and take time to reflect and be in the present moment. During times of retreat, periods of silence were structured into our day. In our non-retreat lives, we were encouraged to carve out periods of silence for ourselves.

- **Study and self-development:** we agreed to make study and learning (about ourselves, as well as about theology and philosophy) a central part of our experience.

- **Service with compassion:** we set ourselves the objective to serve each other and people we encountered in the world with compassion, grace and generosity.

In essence, the 'rules' are high-level principles and values that can be applied in a lot of different ways, in a lot of different contexts, over a long period of time. They can also be inter-preted differently, depending on the individual applying them. And this is an ideal exercise to close out our work together in this chapter, because it gives you a clear set of steps with which to reorganize your life around your personal sense of mean-ing and values. This is where the work starts to become less 'internal' (focusing on you and your position to your life) and more 'external' (in other words: how will you actually choose to live?).

In the following exercise, we'll work through how to create your own rule of life.

EXERCISE 5

Crafting your rule

Take a sheet of paper and start by listing your key personal values and principles. In the Resources section, you'll find a list of suggestions for personal values, so feel free to find inspiration there – but make sure anything you select feels personal to you. Once you have your collection of personal values (there's no limit on how many you can add, but make sure to prioritize your most important ones), you can start to craft your own rule of life.

Begin by taking a single principle: let's say, for example, *generosity*. Perhaps this is one of your key values. Write the word 'generosity' as your heading and add a short paragraph (three or four lines works best) about the importance of this characteristic and how you intend to uphold it. Here's an example of how it could look in practice.

Generosity

Generosity involves giving away my privileges and gifts so that other people can benefit. I practise generosity because I understand my connection to others, and I want to use my talents, abilities and opportunities to help, where I can. I intend to take every chance to be generous, and I will continually look for ways in which I can give back to others.

Once you've completed one principle, repeat with the others. You're aiming for somewhere between seven to ten principles: not too many that it becomes vague and generalized, but not too few that it becomes overly focused on a singular aspect.

Remember, it's *your* rule of life – so make sure you're being honest about the things that matter most to you. Not every principle has to be focused on other people: you can include things like wellbeing, self-care and self-improvement. And as with all of the exercises in this book, you're welcome to return to your rule of life at any time and rewrite or redesign as you feel appropriate.

Before we go on

When it comes to 'self-development', it's easy to overlook the importance of this work. We can see the evidence for maintaining good mental and physical health, and our careers are also obvious things to work on, but the 'self'? Sometimes it can feel too vague, or indulgent, or abstract.

Of course, working on the 'self' has a long history, through different paths and practices: religion, philosophy, self-help, therapy, tradition. The human experience calls for an element of curiosity: what, exactly, are we doing here? How should we navigate our own identity? What should we make of ourselves? These are big questions, for which there is – of course – no obvious or straightforward answer. But the work of this chapter is an invitation: to step into the full experience of being human; to question and observe and reflect; to pay attention to yourself. To refuse to race through your life towards an ever-approaching finish line, but instead to face yourself with care and thoughtfulness. To experiment and try out different things. And this journey, the journey that millions of others have taken before us, ensures that we live fully, stepping into the depths of our lives and discovering what we can learn.

A final note, because – in the process of all that existential contemplation – things got a little intense! Recently, I was speaking at an event about some of the topics and concepts in this book. At the end, someone from the audience came up to introduce himself – a young professional, who had just started out in his first corporate career. He wanted to tell me, he said, that it actually sounded quite exciting, to be exploring and reflecting and mapping out his life and his work and his own identity. He *looked* excited, too. Sometimes you spot these people, the people who are diving into their lives head-first, with open eyes and curiosity and *aliveness*.

My fundamental belief is that this kind of work should be fulfilling and interesting to you despite the challenges. If it starts to feel tiring or irrelevant or boring, rethink it or redesign it until it becomes meaningful. There are as many ways to engage with these questions as there are people on the planet. This is *your* life, after all. Only you get to decide how to go into it fully.

PART III

The Path Ahead

CHAPTER 8

What to Do with All of This

● ● ●

And so, here we are, approaching the end of this introductory
journey into the practice of aliveness. My hope – for myself as
well as for you, the reader – is that this work becomes a personal toolkit, helping you cultivate a sense of deeper 'aliveness'
over time. And, as we explored at the start of this book, the
definition of what it means to be fully 'alive' is up to you. In the
end, aliveness is a subjective experience, and only *you* will be
able to determine whether a practice is working or not.

In this final section, we'll work through a couple of ways to
integrate the ideas of this book into your life. After all, we can
think and reflect and journal on these concepts as much as we
like. The real question is: How will we *live* these ideas? And
ultimately: What will we *do* with all of this?

From theory to practice

So, what is all this for, in the end? With our precious few years
on the planet, and a multitude of ways to spend them, how do
all the exercises and suggestions in this book help us? In this
section, we'll cover a few ways our aliveness-focused work can
be useful in a practical sense, and then we'll look at some everyday methods for integrating the work into our lives.

IF YOU CAME HERE LOOKING FOR INSPIRATION

Perhaps you picked up this book in the hope it would provide you with new ideas, concepts or a different way of thinking (I hope it has!). If you've been searching for inspiration, it's worth diving deeper into the exercises you particularly liked. Many of the practices outlined in this book take time and come with deep, fascinating histories. If you've read about a particular background or tradition that interests you, there's a whole Resources section at the back for you to explore. The self-help genre, in general, doesn't really lend itself to long-term application (to sell a quick-fix, there needs to be a quick solution), but my hope is that this book provides accessible insights and enduring opportunities for transformation over the months and years to come.

IF YOU CAME HERE LOOKING FOR A PROGRAMME FOR DEPTH OR TRANSFORMATION

Many times, I've searched for a particular book to help with a particular challenge. There have been times I've looked for the answer to a question, or for direction, or for help with a personal or professional problem. And there have been times I've looked for depth, meaning and purpose (many times, actually). I love writing books because I am, fundamentally, someone who needs these kinds of books in my life and loves to read them. My hope is that, if you're a searcher like me, this book gives you some starting points for the rest of your journey – a journey that you can really only take alone. So, what should you make of this book? How can you get as much value from the exercises as possible? I'd recommend setting yourself a structured methodology to work through it, and – with that in mind – here's one final exercise for you to try out.

The 30-day aliveness practice

In this practice, you'll use a 30-day period as a structure in which to work through the topics, exercises and disciplines in the book, and you'll draw your experience together with some reflections at the end. As with everything else in the book, you can choose how to bring this practice into your everyday life. Use the template below as a starting point, experiment with what works best, and craft a version of this final exercise that reflects your lifestyle, priorities and preferences.

Before you begin

Gather all of the resources you'll need for the next 30 days. First, this book. And then, a dedicated notebook, folder or journal. Add any other reading that you want to explore (things from the Resources, for example). And map out, on your calendar, when your 30-day period begins and ends.

Day 1

On your first day, make yourself an overall plan. During this practice, you'll be moving through the chapters of the book in a structured, methodological way. Days 2–7 are for your mind, days 8–15 are for your body, days 16–22 are for your work, and days 23–29 are for your self (day 30 is used to conclude your practice). Figure out, using your calendar, which days correspond to which sections and note any points at which you might have to pause the practice (for example: holidays, travel, work or other commitments). If you have big conflicts coming up on your calendar, you can always extend the practice, or shorten it, depending on what works best for you.

Days 2–7

During this period, find a regular slot each day to work through Chapter 4 (Mind). Spend the first few days reading (or re-reading) the chapter and then pick your favourite exercises to try. Dedicate at least 15 minutes a day to reading or working through each exercise. On the seventh day, go back through all of your notes, gather any lessons, observations or wisdom, and store all of your findings in one place.

Days 8–15

During this period, you'll be focused on Chapter 5 (Body). Spend the first few days reading (or rereading) the chapter, and then work through your favourite exercises. Find a regular time in your day to try the physical practices, and take notes or reflections in a way that feels helpful to you. On the fifteenth day, go back through all of your notes, gather anything you've learned, and collect all of your findings in one place.

Days 16–22

Next, revisit Chapter 6 (Work). Spend some time going back through the chapter itself and then pick out the exercises that interest you. This chapter might be easier to integrate into your daily life than the others – it has a professional focus (you can justify doing this work as part of your professional development!), so you might be able to dedicate a little more time to it each day. On the twenty-second day, go back through your notes, gather your findings, and add it all to your collection from the previous days.

Days 23–29

Last up, Chapter 7 (Self). This – in my opinion – is the most challenging element, and the part where this work gets really personal. Try to carve out enough time in your day to really give the exercises the space and resources they require. You can always extend the practice by a few days if you're enjoying the process, needing more time, or finding it particularly fulfilling. On your final day, go back through all of your notes from this chapter, gather everything you've discovered or explored, and add it to your notebook or folder.

Day 30

When you choose to end the practice, create a closing session. Assemble all of your notes, reflections and findings from the exercises, and go back through them. Look for key themes, lessons, pieces of advice or wisdom that you can take forwards with you. You can refine and restructure your notes however you like – and keep returning to them, as you continue this work over time. The 30 days are intended to kickstart your personal practice, but – as we all know by now – this is ongoing (lifelong!) work. Whenever you forget, you can just pick up where you left off.

One final thing, before you close out your 30-day practice. Decide *now*, before you finish, how this work will take shape in your life for the next 30 days (and the 30 days after that). Which practices do you want to keep? Which ones will you leave behind? How will you hold yourself accountable and keep yourself on track? As ever, these questions – and the very act of asking them – are more important than the answers, which will evolve and develop over time.

IF YOU CAME HERE LOOKING FOR PRACTICAL EXERCISES TO GET STARTED

Moments of enlightenment are often fleeting. One moment you're experiencing deep, personal transformation, the next you're running to catch a bus or standing in the line at the supermarket. As much as we value those moments of realization and connection, we can't linger in that space for too long. We have to go back *into* our lives, because there are things we need to do, tasks we need to finish, projects we need to push forwards and, ultimately (and more excitingly), change we need to make in the world. But it's tempting to cling to those moments of change and growth, getting stuck at the point of transformation, and then use that as an excuse to go right back to our everyday lives *unchanged*. (I'm sure you can imagine a few people like this – people who have done the deep, personal, even spiritual work, but returned to their daily lives without any lasting change to their character or behaviour.) It's one thing to experience personal, inner growth and development, but the hardest work of all might be the moment at which we take our new wisdom back into the world and apply it to the ordinary, everyday routines of our lives.

I've experienced this before, a moment of 'spiritual connection' (or, to put it more simply, a personal insight or realization) slipping through my fingers as soon as I got back into everyday life. Several occasions, returning from a long monastic retreat, I'd be on the train on the way home, checking my emails, feeling totally separated from the spiritual transformation that I'd just felt so closely connected to. Being in a monastic community is one thing. It's more straightforward to feel like a spiritually connected, compassionate person when you're head-to-toe in white robes, chanting prayers in a room full of monks. The real challenge (and this applies to everyone, not just monks) is in *holding on* to all the new things you learned and experienced, even in the middle of your most annoying, boring, frustrating days (*especially* in the middle of those days, in fact).

How, then, can we do this? I have a few suggestions: things that have worked for me, and things I've learned from others. You can keep your own list as well, and add to it over time – this is a personal challenge, and my struggles will be different from yours. But try things out; experiment with your life. You only get one opportunity, after all. You might as well.

1. Keeping a regular writing practice

One of the most popular writing practices around is named 'Morning Pages'. Morning Pages are a tool created by author Julia Cameron and originally intended to support a creative practice (Morning Pages are part of Cameron's structured guidebook, *The Artist's Way*[1]). To complete Morning Pages, there are just a couple of rules: first, write early; second, write by hand; and third, stop after three pages (according to Cameron, this last rule is '*to avoid self-involvement and narcissism*'). The key to Morning Pages is writing *freely* – you write, as much as you want, as fast as you want, for your three pages, and then you stop. There's evidence behind this practice, too: studies indicate that reflective writing can benefit the immune system (although the effect varies, depending on duration of practice and the individual writer).[2]

Reflective writing – either Morning Pages or a similar practice – can be a helpful tool for putting some of our work into action. Writing practices can keep you on a consistent track, keep you aware of your own progress (especially if you revisit your previous writing to reflect on changes over time), and – most importantly – keep you connected to yourself. By committing to sit with yourself, every day (or thereabouts), with a pen and paper, you're much more likely to stay present in your own life. A writing practice can keep you dedicated to your personal development, and it can also anchor you *here*, in the present moment, showing up to each day and facing it head on.

In the context of the work of this book, you might like to try Morning Pages (or a version of this practice): you could, for example, explore Morning Pages as a way of reflecting on the exercises you're trying out. Or, you can mix in a writing practice with another exercise from this book. For example, if you end your day with a body scan practice (Chapter 5), you could make a few written notes or reflections about how it felt, or any changes you noticed over time. If you're working through your portfolio career design (Chapter 6), or through some of the meaning-focused practices (Chapter 4), you can bring in an element of reflective writing – either for brainstorming ideas, or for noting a few reflections on how helpful you found the exercise.

For those who like to stay organized, you could even designate a separate notebook or folder to collect all of the writing practices and notes that you create as you work through this book. That way, you can approach a topic that seems a bit intimidating (such as – for example – your own existence) in a way that feels practical and grounded in reality.

2. Finding an advisor, mentor or other supporter

It's easy to see the importance of having someone on our team, someone who will support us unconditionally on the journey towards our goals. It's not always obvious, though, that we should be finding advisors, mentors or supporters for *this* type of work – the work of figuring out our own lives. Often, this work feels deeply personal, and it's not straightforward to find someone who both understands our path *and* has the expertise and wisdom that we need. Having said that, many of the practices and traditions in this book advocate for finding a support system. In the Ignatian monastic tradition, the work of the *Spiritual Exercises* is designed to be completed alongside a spiritual director. In the yoga tradition, the practice is grounded in the teacher–student relationship. And in more clinical topics like logotherapy (or the path to finding meaning), the journey is supported by therapists, counsellors or other advisors.

All of these options are open to you, of course: you could find yourself a teacher, guide, spiritual director, therapist or other specifically trained expert to help you explore a particular practice. But it can also be a little simpler. As you're working through the practices, look around you at the people who embody the qualities you're working towards. Clarity of purpose; physical presence and embodiment; a carefully crafted career; a sense of self-awareness: whatever it is, look for people who seem to have it. And then, once you've located them, figure out how you can learn from them. If it's someone you know well, invite them to chat to you over coffee – tell them what you admire in them, and ask them for their wisdom. How, exactly, did they cultivate that quality in themselves over time? As we've explored so often in this book, many of these qualities, characteristics or personality traits are *learned* and *practised*, rather than gifted or inherent. Everyone has their own methodologies for moving through the world, so if someone inspires you, see if they can teach you something. If your inspiration isn't someone in your close circle, figure out how you can stay updated on their work. If they're a writer, sign up to their newsletter, or gather your own collection of their publications. If they're a speaker, become a regular at their talks and events. You don't need to have close, personal contact with someone in order for them to teach or guide you. You can learn from a distance.

Finally, remember that mentoring and advisory relationships are only effective – at least in the long run – if you put the work in over time. Having one coffee with someone you admire is great, but there's a risk of just noting down their advice in your mind and moving on with your life unchanged. If you want to utilize the mentoring or advisory relationship fully, make it your responsibility to learn, to gain something from every interaction. Take notes, figure out practical steps, put them into action. Reflect on how the advice changed you and your life. If you're in contact with your mentor, feed back to them, and keep the conversation going. Over time, notice whether their advice still applies, or if you need to find a new set of mentors for the next stage of your path. As always, the work is ongoing, flexible and ever-evolving.

3. Collecting visual or physical reminders

Humans have long used physical objects to represent personal meaning. From wedding rings to tattoos, from lucky charms to religious symbols: when we can *see* something, we can be reminded of the importance, meaning and values behind it. We remember why we were doing our work in the first place, or what it was we were fighting for. When I began my training in a monastic community, we were all given wooden crosses. The idea was to carry these crosses around – in our pockets or backpacks – as a physical reminder of the priorities we'd set for ourselves. Many people wore them around the neck, as a way to stay physically anchored to the symbol.

This idea doesn't have to be as dramatic as a big wooden cross, though. Vision boards, laptop backgrounds, passwords that trigger a certain memory – there are an endless number of ways to make this concept work for you. Wherever you are in the process of the work of this book, find a visual reminder that represents that point. For example, if you're working on the meaning-focused questions (Chapter 4), you could pick a favourite meaning-related quote to set as your phone lockscreen. Or, if you're working on the body-focused practices (Chapter 5), you could write the word 'presence' or 'embodiment' on a note and place it somewhere you'll notice it each day. When you choose your physical or visual reminders, you're looking to find something that you see *every now and then*. Too frequent, and it will merge into the background of your environment. Too infrequent, and you might forget about it altogether. Again, and as always, experiment to see what works best for you.

CHAPTER 9

Frequently Asked Questions:
Some Things You Might Be Wondering

• • •

What if I don't feel more fully 'alive', even after doing all of the exercises in this book?

Let's come back to the definition of 'aliveness' that we explored at the start of this book. We talked about aliveness from a few perspectives – both internal (your personal experience) and external (the way you perceive others). But, in the end, aliveness is a subjective, individual question. I can't promise you that any tool, technique, teacher or book is going to give you a perfect result (and you should be very wary of those that do promise it!). After all, our subjective experience of life is always changing. You might feel a sense of aliveness one day and lose it the next. You might have a few years of feeling fully present, connected and inspired, and a few years of feeling lost.

There's no way to do this work correctly – or incorrectly. My hope is just that you started (or continued) a journey, a journey that only you can shape for yourself. If you don't feel any different after working through all of the practices in this book, go deeper – check out the Resources, explore different traditions, read more books(!), learn from more teachers. Only you can decide what works, and how, and why. Let your life be the process of figuring it out. (And, to put it frankly, the very fact you read this book – all the way to the FAQs section! – indicates that you're far more present, curious and – yes – *fully alive* than you might think.)

I'm not religious or spiritual. How should I use these practices?

Obviously, some of these practices (monasticism, for example, or Sabbath) belong to certain traditions, and those *specific* practices should be performed in a way that honours and respects their context. Having said that, the practices themselves still offer us opportunities to learn, grow and change our own behaviour in a way that can give our life greater depth and meaning. If you want to read more about the practices themselves, including the historical background, head to the Resources section.

Remember: if you are extracting ideas from historical, traditional, cultural or religious practices, it's the *core teachings* or *wisdom* that you should be using as education and insight for your own life. This is a different approach to extracting an entire cultural practice and dropping it directly into a different context. Fundamentally, during any work with other traditions, ideas and teachings, your intention should always be one of respect, openness, curiosity, intelligence and appreciation.

I'd prefer to adopt a single tradition or practice and use that as my entire focus. Is that in line with the thinking in this book?

Absolutely. These practices are just offerings, and if you find one that particularly connects with you, head straight to the Resources section and dive in to learn more.

What if I'm too tired or busy to put this stuff into action?

The world can be exhausting. Between careers and families and relationships and socializing and exercising and posting on social media, we barely have a second to catch our breath, let alone delve into this kind of work. Right?

Well, yes – but this might be part of the problem. We're encouraged to move fast through the world, constructing our lives according to predetermined plans and achieving things to impress others, and we rarely stop and question why we're actually doing it. And, importantly, question whether the choices we carry out on autopilot are actually the ones we'd select for ourselves, if we sat down with a blank piece of paper and a spare hour or two. The risk is, of course, that we wake up one Monday morning a decade later and wonder how we ended up there, and where all the time went.

My intention with this book is to make the work both accessible and practical. By splitting up the exercises separately, and giving you the ability to pick and choose from a selection of options, it might be easier to carve out time when you can find it. A word of caution, though – these exercises are most effective if you can bring a level of awareness and attention to them. Twenty minutes spent in full concentration on an exercise is likely to be more effective than an hour multitasking your way through it.

One practical strategy is to see this work as an important part of your 'self-care' routine. Realistically, this might mean replacing something else that you currently do, but you don't have to make it a dramatic input of time. I strongly believe you should also *enjoy* working through the practices, and focus on the ones that resonate most with your lifestyle and preferences.

Remember, too, that this work will spill over and impact other areas of your life, so it's never just a one-time contribution of energy. Instead, it's more like an investment – make an initial payment of time and you'll find the benefits return to you, with regularity, over the following weeks, months and years.

I'd like to take a break. Do we always have to be searching for 'full aliveness'?

In short, no. We don't always have to be focused fully on this work, and – just like any other practice in your life – it's fine to pause. A couple of thoughts, as you decide to take your break:

- Try to make any decision to pause with awareness. Deciding to step back deliberately is often a good choice, if you feel you need it. But stepping back through complacency, apathy or overwhelm can be a warning sign, rather than a self-care initiative. If you feel like you're having to take a break from your life because it just seems too much to handle, it's a good idea to re-evaluate, and/or speak to a professional about it, if helpful.

- Sometimes, this kind of work – for example, working through questions of meaning and purpose – can be difficult for other reasons. Perhaps it feels stressful to reflect on your experiences, or perhaps you just don't want to address certain aspects of your life. There's nothing in this work that compels you to do things a certain way: the benefit of the approach in this book is that you can pick and choose your favourite practices. You can also redesign the practices, using the frameworks suggested, to create something that works for you. (If there is something in your life that feels like a significant block to self-reflection, or an issue that you feel would benefit from some assistance, it might be a good idea to speak to a professional about it.)

Is becoming more 'alive' to life likely to result in more awareness of our challenges and difficulties?

Unfortunately, it might – but this isn't necessarily a bad thing! Life isn't ever as perfect as our Instagram feeds might like to make out. Struggles, challenges and difficulties are part of the texture of our human existence – and, in some ways, they're the very things that make our lives intense, deep and full. If we had a filtered, flawless existence, there wouldn't be that much to *feel*. The 'negative' parts of life belong, just as much as everything else. The challenge is, at the most fundamental level, whether we can navigate the negative parts with presence, intention and integrity. This is where the real work of *finding aliveness* lies, within the full spectrum of human experience.

I already feel fully alive. How can I best use the practices in this book?

Congratulations! I hope this book can be an additional tool to support and enhance the depth, meaning and purpose you've already discovered. The path towards a more fulfilled experience of being human is infinite: in other words, when it comes to the topic of feeling *fully alive*, I believe we can never get too much.

Resources

• • •

Introduction

1 https://www.bls.gov/news.release/tenure.nr0.htm
2 https://www.bls.gov/news.release/pdf/nlsoy.pdf (Which puts things into perspective somewhat, especially if you – like me – were feeling nervous about leaving a first career behind!)
3 The 'existential vacuum', a term developed by Viktor Frankl, was originally used to describe a feeling of meaninglessness or emptiness. Its main manifestation was in boredom – think of, for example, the feeling on Sunday afternoons when the week's work is paused for a moment. What then? What's the meaning of your life when you slow down enough to think about it? Frankl thought that this was, perhaps, something particular to the twentieth century, perhaps as a result of the decline in social traditions (in a previous generation, Sundays might, in Western cultures, have been set aside for religious gatherings or other community activities). Anyway, as you can imagine, this is all still relevant for us today.
4 For the purposes of this book, this is a generalized term and not the name of a specific field. From a technical perspective, we'll be covering 'logotherapy' and 'Existential Analysis'.
5 If you Google the word 'phenomenology', Wikipedia will tell you that phenomenology 'is not a unified movement; rather, the works of different authors who share a 'family resemblance' but with many significant differences'. Needless to say, we won't be attempting to use a set definition in our work here – instead, we'll just look to the concept for ideas, inspiration and wisdom. For more detail on phenomenology (and in particular, its application to psychology and existentialism), try Spinelli's *The Interpreted World*, 1989 (SAGE Publications).

RESOURCES

Chapter 1

1 If you are too young to know what an emoticon is, that really proves the point.
2 https://learnmore.monster.com/poll-results-from-work-in-the-time-of-coronavirus and https://www.flexjobs.com/employer-blog/companies-prevent-employee-burnout-during-pandemic/ (These are obviously difficult features to measure in the context of a research study, so perhaps the true figures are even greater.)

Chapter 2

1 These statistics have been quoted all over the place, including in *The New York Times* and *The Guardian*, and are supposedly from a Microsoft Consumer Insights study in 2015. The BBC later cast some doubt on the origin, suggesting they were cited in Microsoft's report but were actually derived from a different source called 'Statistic Brain'. (In any event, if you made it all the way to the end of this paragraph, your personal attention span is probably just fine.)
2 https://www.ncbi.nlm.nih.gov/pmc/articles/PMC3004979/
3 This technique was apparently described by Taiichi Ohno at Toyota Motor Corporation, in the context of manufacturing.

Chapter 3

1 This idea, and related topics, are discussed in depth in Frankl's '*Yes to Life*', from 1946 (Beacon Press).
2 https://news.stanford.edu/2005/06/14/jobs-061505/ (Notice, in particular, the final line about creativity, which often gets cut off when this quote is passed around social media platforms.)
3 Maslow's work is complex, and requires a separate, fuller examination. For an in-depth exploration of the topic, try psychologist Scott Barry Kaufman's *Transcend*, 2020 (TarcherPerigee).
4 According to Viktor Frankl's grandson, Alexander Vesely, in an interview recorded in Parabola (https://parabola.org/2017/01/31/viktor-frankl-and-the-search-for-meaning-a-conversation-with-alexander-vesely-and-mary-cimiluca/). For a fuller perspective, see the evolution of Maslow's

work as explored in *Transcend* by Scott Barry Kaufman, 2020 (TarcherPerigee).

Chapter 4

1 Of course, this is not a clinical or therapeutic book, and is not designed to treat specific mental health concerns. If you're looking for something more specific, there are some great resource lists on the NHS website (for UK readers), at Mind, or the National Institute of Mental Health.

2 At the time of writing, there were 130 logotherapy institutes in the world, in 41 countries.

3 Much of this work draws on teachings from the Viktor Frankl Institute of Ireland, and in particular the work of Dr Stephen J. Costello (Ph.D), the Institute's founder and director. For more on this work, and for recommendations for further study and resources, visit www.viktorfranklireland.com

4 For Frankl's work, the following are recommended: *Man's Search for Meaning*, 1946 (Beacon Press), *The Doctor and the Soul*, 1946 (Knopf), *The Unheard Cry for Meaning*, 1979 (Touchstone) and *Recollections: An Autobiography*, 1997 (Basic Books). For books covering Frankl's work, try books authored by Elizabeth Lukas.

5 As quoted by Frankl in *Man's Search for Meaning*, and originally paraphrased from Nietzsche's *Twilight of the Idols* (1889) 'Maxims and Arrows'.

6 According to the Viktor Frankl Institute, the origin is somewhat complicated (in short, the author Stephen R. Covey had stated he discovered the quote in a library and thought it aligned with Frankl's views – but the details of the book were not recounted): https://www.viktorfrankl.org/quote_stimulus.html

7 Each school of teaching has its own nuanced views on this point, but the core of most practices tends towards self transcendence.

8 Daniel Kahneman, *Thinking, Fast and Slow*, 2011 (Farrar, Straus and Giroux).

9 For more on mysticism, with a focus on Christian traditions, see the work of the Center for Action and Contemplation (https://cac.org/themes/introduction-to-christian-mysticism/).

10 See, for example, Book 12 of the *De Trinitate*.

Chapter 5

1 https://globalwellnessinstitute.org/industry-research/the-global-wellness-economy-looking-beyond-covid/

2 There are a few sources this could be derived from (Eckhart Tolle's teaching on totality of presence, for example, or Tara Brach's meditations on full body awareness).

3 Bessel van der Kolk, *The Body Keeps the Score: Mind, Brain, and Body in the Transformation of Trauma*, 2015 (Penguin).

4 Jon Kabat-Zinn, *Full Catastrophe Living: Using the Wisdom of Your Body and Mind to Face Stress, Pain, and Illness*, 2013 (Bantam).

5 Jon Kabat-Zinn, *Full Catastrophe Living: Using the Wisdom of Your Body and Mind to Face Stress, Pain, and Illness*, 2013 (Bantam).

6 For more on alignment, try *The Pilates Bible* by Robinson, Bradshaw and Gardner, 2019 (Kyle Books), or *Pilates Anatomy* by Isacowitz and Clippinger, 2019 (Human Kinetics).

7 https://www.ucl.ac.uk/hbrc/diet/lallyp.html (This number is relentlessly disputed. Let's settle on a good couple of months, to be sure.)

8 For more on this, see: *Yoga Sutras of Patañjali*, by Sri Swami Satchidananda, republished in 2012 (Integral Yoga Publications).

9 https://www.fastcompany.com/90354456/these-navy-seal-tricks-will-help-you-perform-better-under-pressure (Reportedly...).

10 See, for example: https://www.health.harvard.edu/mind-and-mood/relaxation-techniques-breath-control-helps-quell-errant-stress-response

11 For an exploration of this idea, see Richard Rohr's *The Naked Now: Learning to See as the Mystics See*, 2009 (The Crossroad Publishing Company).

12 The concept of Existential Fundamental Motivation (and 'fundamental trust') is derived from the work of the leading existential psychotherapist Alfried Längle. For example, see *The Art of Involving the Person*, 2003 (European Psychotherapy).

13 This exercise draws on similar approaches from Existential Analysis and other fields (in Existential Analysis, a similar exercise is referred to as 'the armchair exercise', and there are similar practices in other schools of psychotherapy).

Chapter 6

1 Charles Handy, *The Age of Unreason*, 1995 (Random House Business).
2 Charles Handy, *The Age of Unreason*, 1995 (Random House Business).
3 There are lots of books that cover this topic – try Héctor García's *Ikigai: The Japanese Secret to a Long and Happy Life*, 2017 (Hutchinson).
4 Viktor Frankl, *The Doctor and the Soul*, 1946 (Knopf).

Chapter 7

1 Included in *Gratitude*, a collection of essays written by Oliver Sacks during the last few months of his life (early version published in 2015 by Knopf).
2 For more on the concept of liminality, try *Liminality and the Modern: Living Through the In-Between* by Bjørn Thomassen, 2014 (Routledge).
3 If you're interested, there are a few books you can use to dive deeper – try *A Celebration of Customs and Rituals Around the World* by Ingpen & Wilkinson, 1996 (Facts on File Inc.).
4 Epictetus, *Discourses*, written around 108 ad (Penguin Classics).
5 On a similar topic, you could explore the Buddhist approach to meditation on death, which is called *Maranasati* (mindfulness of death).
6 Marcus Aurelius, *Meditations Book 3.1*, written around 180 ad (Benediction Classics), reformulated translation by Stoic teacher Kathryn Koromilas.
7 For more on this tradition, you could start with the resources available from the Ignatian Spirituality Center (https://www.ignatiancenter.org/ignatianresources). The original analysis is explored in the *Spiritual Exercises of St Ignatius of Loyola*, written around 1522.
8 https://link.springer.com/article/10.1007/s10902-020-00236-6 (Yes, behind all the cliches and Instagram quotes, there might be something worth holding on to.)

Chapter 8

1 Viktor Frankl, *Man's Search for Meaning*, 1946 (Beacon Press).

Chapter 9

1 Julia Cameron, *The Artist's Way*, 1992 (TarcherPerigee).
2 https://www.apa.org/monitor/jun02/writing (A similar idea is the field of 'embodied cognition', in which emotions and thoughts in the mind can have real, tangible impacts in the physical body. As we've been discovering this whole time, everything is integrated.)

A CHECKLIST OF VALUES

- Freedom
- Openness
- Authenticity
- Growth
- Giving
- Balance
- Honesty
- Integrity
- Attention to detail
- Challenge
- Creativity
- Reputation
- Collaboration
- Independence
- Community
- Influence
- Security
- Flexibility
- Affluence
- Competition

- Innovation
- Self-awareness
- Consistency
- Solitude
- Spirituality
- Intellect
- Structure
- Fluidity
- Diversity
- Inclusion
- Leadership
- Wisdom
- Learning
- Equality
- Teamwork
- Experimentation
- Loyalty
- Faith
- Curiosity
- Humility

Acknowledgements

• • •

One of my father's favourite quotes is (somewhat unexpectedly) from a Roman playwright known as Terence (brought to Rome by senator Terentius Lucanus, and who later became a famous writer – around 170 BCE). The quote is:

"Homo sum, humani nihil a me alienum puto"

Which roughly translates as: *"I am human, I consider nothing that is human alien to me."*

This depth and inclusivity of human experience is, of course, one of the central ideas behind the work in this book (and behind my own journey into deeper 'aliveness'), and so – thanks, Dad.

And to my family – I'm so grateful for all the support, encouragement, inspiration, and endless questions about when this book will be finally out. Here it is!

To Jaime, for being my companion, reviewer, guide and general provider of wisdom. To everyone who read and reflected on early drafts – thank you. And to Jonathan and the team at John Murray: thank you for believing in the book, and for helping me bring it into existence!

To every tutor, teacher, guide, author, monk, spiritual leader, instructor, mystic and creator that has inspired the content of this book (of whom there are many), and to those I am yet to encounter (hopefully many more) – thank you.